Conversation with Angels

Conversation with Angels

AND SO BE IT

Dror B. Ashuah

EPIGRAPH
A DIVISION OF MONKFISH BOOK PUBLISHING COMPANY
RHINEBECK ~ NEW YORK

ISBN 9780979882883

Book and cover design by Georgia Dent

Library of Congress Control Number: 2008941269

Bulk purchase discounts for educational or promotional purposes are available.

First Edition

First Impression

10987654321

To continue the conversation: WWW.ANDSOBEIT.COM

Epigraph
An Alternative Publishing Imprint of
Monkfish Book Publishing Company
27 Lamoree Road
Rhinebeck, New York 12572
www.epigraphps.com

Contents

Foreword

THE ANGELS TELL US that earth is going through a monumental shift. Our collective consciousness is going through a vibrational shift as if we were attuned to one radio station and the dial were turning to another. Much of what we assume to be true today is about to change. All of us are about to transform as well, and the angels ask us to get ready.

These messages are for you, the angels say, for you came to earth at this time to gain mastery over yourself and discover your own divinity. By shining your light, you fulfill your mission to dispel darkness in these exciting yet tumultuous times. You signed up for this mission, agreeing to act as a lighthouse, shining your light and showing those lost at sea a path to a safe harbor. Now an alarm clock sounds, and there is no snooze button to punch. *Wake up!* It is time. Wake up to your purpose and allow your divinity to emanate from your being and become the light that you are. That is the heart of this book's message and purpose.

The angels tell us that the words in this book act as a conveyor of love energy from the circle. Their message prompts us to awaken our latent memories buried deep in our cellular structure. You do not need to understand every concept. This book needs to be felt more than intellectualized. They tell us that these messages activate your feeling centers to awaken your innate knowing and to develop your feminine aspect so you can manifest your multidimensional being and manifest healing, balance, peace, abundance and joy in your life.

Who am I to deliver this message? I have no simple answer. I am a human being who happens to be male with typical worries: responsibilities, family life, bills. In 1997 my wife gave birth to our daughter during the time that I completed my graduate work at Harvard in psychology and human development. Both my wife, a visual artist, and I were deeply embedded in the realm of manifesting, creating, developing a business, traveling, juggling duties, and in short being busy in the dance of life. This dance continued for a few more years.

And then something happened in May of 2000 that threw me off my busy trajectory. My close friend from high school suddenly died from an infection from a minor surgery. He was healthy, smart, and creative. He had a wife and one child like me, and he was spiritual and always seemed joyous. He wasn't — in my scheme of things — *supposed* to die. His death did not make sense. I was unable to reconcile it and began to search. I felt that there was something hidden behind his death, and I was determined to find out what it was.

I did not talk to anyone about his death, nor did I hire a detective. Instead, I began to read. I started reading books on anything I could find from spirituality to Eastern and Western philosophy to discover answers to my questions about life's purpose. The more I read, the more I wanted to find out. Gradually, I became peaceful with his loss. I discovered a clue and began to follow it. The search allowed me to find more peace and love inside of me, and I felt that I was slowly changing.

Through her art and her yearning to explore her own spiritual side, my wife guided us to China, Japan, Peru, the Amazon, India, and other parts of the world where pieces of the puzzle, of why we humans are here and what our purpose is, came closer together to form a more complete picture. In 2003 we moved to New York City from Boston after selling our business, and while there I was freer to pursue my spiritual studies, meditate, and move more deeply inside.

I was in the metropolitan hub of life seeking stillness. We cooked at home, became vegetarians, meditated regularly, and reduced our busy social life. After returning from a trip to Japan where we spent considerable time meditating in the temples of Kyoto, my wife felt that she wanted to try to live in Europe for a short time while tending to her elderly parents. I stayed in New York City to wrap up some things before joining them.

Suddenly, all was quiet. I continued to meditate, to balance myself, and I could feel that my body was vibrating differently. In one morning meditation, I felt as if I did not need to breathe anymore. I was breathing through my skin. At times after meditation my body would vibrate inside as if I were a light soap bubble sitting on a washing machine.

Then, one day in December 2007, while meditating, I heard this voice.

This joyful, happy-go-lucky voice said for me to go to the computer and just wait and let go. So I turned on the computer and waited. "That sounds easy," I thought. And then I heard the beginning of a sentence, and then I heard the next sentence, and then I just kept following and typing what I heard. I wasn't worried about what I was going to write or what was being said. I just let it be written. When I read it again, it was a short paragraph that gave me an intention to be in a place of love so I could be ready to write.

After this short experience, I felt light and wonderful; so, I went to have tea at Starbucks on Reade Street and

Broadway to try to process the event. While sitting there, I had a vision of three angels. And I "heard" the first message and took notes. That was on December 10th 2007.

And then two hours passed! I tried to read the message, and it sounded strange yet beautiful. It came without effort and with love, joy, and peace.

I continued. For each of the next several days for six months, two hours almost each day, I worked with this same process of receiving and writing. Each time I wrote, I had to be in a place of no judgment. I had to let it flow. While taking notes I would often be shown visions that I cannot describe, smell scents that I do not have names for, and see geometric shapes that I cannot even draw. Even if the message came without a clear ending or with a clear sense of where it was taking me, I just kept letting one word lead me to the next word. The process was an act of faith. The greatest challenge was not to hold on to any pre-conceptions of anything—of reality or even how a sentence should be constructed. Every time before taking down the message I would read the intention and wait to hear the first word or sentence.

The process was similar for each of the messages. Like a student in class I would write what I heard. At times I experienced fears that the messengers would not come back, but they always did.

I had to surrender. It was a new experience, but it always felt light and joyful. The messages started to bring clarity to my life and my own challenges. Whereas I might normally lose balance from a daily challenge, instead I stayed centered. At times I would get a particular teaching, and the test would come that same day. I would almost smile and tell myself, "At least you cannot claim you weren't told."

Was I "channeling?" I wondered and asked the angels to give me a clue. They gave me their version of the source of information on October 2, 2008. I included it in "Forward from the Angels" at the beginning of the book. Their version was fascinating to me, and I urge you to read it. The messages included in this book are from December 10, 2007 until March 1, 2008. There are over 40 messages from March to October 2008, which will be published in a second volume. I continue to write their messages as they come.

The process of taking notes and allowing these messages to come to light was both humbling and a great honor. I do not presume to know more than you, and I do not presume to be able to explain all of it. I was given a task to be a clear vessel that allows the energy of love and light to come through me to reach you. I do not see myself as a teacher but as a student.

The angels tell me that you the reader have asked for and actually manifested this book. They tell me that this information is not new to us and that we already know everything written here. They tell us that they are here just to remind us of our divinity and nudge us to remember our mission and shine our light.

This book is meant to be read like a recipe book. Flip through the Message Guide portion in the end of the book. Scan it and whatever paragraph seems to draw your attention, go to that message. This book has the spirit of the circle and is not meant to be read in a linear fashion. Trust that you read what you need to know for this very moment.

These messages work magic for me. The angels tell me that this book is a bridge between our reality and theirs and by just reading it things will begin to shift in our lives. They certainly shifted in mine. They ask you to trust the process and allow it to flow. Know that you are always loved and never judged and know that you are a divine angel and a master of your own life. Know that the time is now for you to wake up to your mission and shine your light and so be it.

IN MEMORY OF OFER FRANK

Foreword from the Angels

W E LOVE YOU SO and this is just the beginning. We come to you in this form because you have asked us to bring this information to you. Some of you may ask, *but where is it coming from, really?*

Our simple answer is that this information is coming from the circle. Some of you may ask if this is what some call channeling. With all love we wish to tell you that many of you misunderstand the idea behind channeling. You are all channeling all the time. It is your linear perception which keeps you from the awareness that you are many things and in many places simultaneously.

Channeling from where we sit, is becoming clear enough to realize the source of the information you are receiving. Like your modern day radio, if you turn into a FM station that transmits classical music, you will say now I am tuned to that station. Now, when you change the station to classic Rock, you will know that indeed you have changed the station. The channeller knows which station she is receiving the message from and can tune to it at will. With all love we wish to tell you that in your day to day life, many of you are exposed to so much noise that you are not walking in the awareness of the circle. It requires you to be in a subtle place to know which music comes from which station.

You are a vessel and that is your mission. It is you who must allow the energy of divinity through so you can become the unlimited multidimensional being that you are. Indeed there are some who channel a particular being from the other side bringing forth specific information. This is not the source of this information. We are angels and we are part of you. You are a group and we are part of your group. You may say to us *yes, but you said that you come from here and there and you do this and that.* Yes, we do and so do you.

You are much larger than you can ever imagine and your group is busy in creating things that you can not even grasp. This information is coming from a source that is in you. *"What if we do not get this information and it does not resonate?* some of you may wonder. With a hug we wish to impart to you that if this information does not resonate with you, know that there is never a judgment, but it is not coming from you and therefore it is not for you. We ask you then to celebrate your diversity and the grandness of your circle and keep searching for your mission. It is never a one size fits all. You all have missions but they are all suited perfectly for each one of you. The ones who were meant to read these messages will know it immediately and without a doubt.

The simple explanation is that you are linear and this information comes from the circle. It connects to the circular part in you. Those of you who created this information will feel that these words resonate fully with your being. Those who will resonate are the creators and the information although brought through one human is meant to allow the many to shift vibration. There are many layers to each of the messages. Each message is meant to address an angel at a particular time on their journey. In essence all of the messages combined are just like an alarm clock. They are meant to wake you up on the cellular level to what you already know and remind you that it is time to get out of bed. You have chosen us to bring this to you and not vise versa. You are the creator and when you go to the store and ask to purchase an alarm clock, the store's clerk hands you one. We are the store's clerk and we follow your request. *But who are you?*, some of you may persist. We are part of you the reader.

We wish to take you by the hand and ask you to fly with us into the magical land of the circle. There, there is no time and no space like the one you occupy on earth. All is multilayered and happens simultaneously. The messages must come through one that has achieved harmonious resonance and a high frequency so the messages can flow with out much distortion. There are always limitations to the messages as they are being delivered through words, and use the vocabulary of the one who transcribes it.

With a hug we wish to tell you that the real purpose of the message is for you to wake up yourself to your own potential. Many of you may say:" *I like this message and I do not like that message. This is from a channel but this is more scientific and it is from the writer's knowledge.*" We ask you to not place boxes around the circle. The source is you. You can put it in the hand of the author or an entity, or you can attribute it to this being or that being but it is you and you will know it fully when you read them.

We love you and we wish to tell you that you are the author and you will know it because it will feel as if you could have written it. It will feel so familiar. We also told you with a hug that these messages are not meant for all of you. If you are not the "author" you will know it as well and there is never a judgment. It does not mean that you are not spiritual enough or divine enough. It only means that you are on a different mission and you may want to keep searching for that which resonates with your mission. You are all angels, all divine and all are on missions. No mission is more honorable or prestigious than the next. You are so dearly loved and we ask you to become that which you are: a master in disguise walking with the knowledge of your own divinity.

The writer, editor and publisher of these messages are simply your messengers as they cater to your intent, bringing you that which you have requested. Do not look at the typeface, the format or the book cover as they are just tools. These messages act as a conveyor of the energy of love which aims to link you with you and to wake you up to your own divinity.

With a hug we wish to impart to you that Love energy acts and harmonizes with your cells facilitating healing in your body when it is appropriate. It is again, not the tools which heal you but it is you who heals yourself through intent. We wish to tell you that these messages do not come from an entity or a channel; they come from you the reader. They come to those of you who requested them. Those who requested them will be guided to these messages and will know instantly that it is for them. Those of you who did not ask for these messages will not be able to finish a single page as it will appear alien or too confusing.

You are magnificent and we see you as geometric patterns moving about; these messages correspond to your geometry and each message links to a moment in time in the cycle you call human life. We ask you to read this book like a recipe book. When you crave a certain type of food, look through the menu and pick the one that seems the most appetizing. Use your feeling and allow the correct message to present itself. Be playful and allow that which comes from the circle to celebrate with you the shifting of you and the planet. You are changing and the planet is changing. Your vibration is increasing and the molecules around you dance differently than they used to.

It is the grandest time in your history as humans on this planet and nothing you know will stay the same. All must shift with the shifting of your planet. It is your intent that gave the push for this change and we ask you to become peaceful with all that is around you. We ask you to use love in all your interactions and relationships. We ask you to become the master that you are at every moment that you breathe. There are many who await your awakening.

There are trillions of us who support your journey and celebrate every light that shines with its own divinity. We ask you to be in the now and know that there is no other time then the time you are in and with a sweet touch we ask you to wake up to your divinity and wear the outfit of the master as it is calling you. And so be it.

December 10th 2007

IT WAS THE FIRST TIME I had left my peaceful apartment the whole day. As I stepped outside, I was carried away by a crowd with umbrellas and large coats, a stream of people negotiating left and right to make their way and still not collide with anyone. It smelled fresh from the light rain that had just begun.

I was walking on Broadway Street and behind me was a French couple pointing to the tip of the City Hall building. I always wondered, with all the beautiful buildings in Europe, what would impress Europeans visiting New York City. Christmas was around the corner and I could feel the energy of excitement and holiday shopping buzz all around me. Then I noticed the scaffolding on the corner of Broadway and Reade Street where the Starbucks coffee shop was. There was a black man dressed in all white with thick black curly hair. He was hiding from the rain under the canopy of the scaffolding. There was something about him that seemed unreal or out of context. His shoes were white and he had the kind of loose dress that one associates with the holy man of India. He noticed my stare and smiled at me with his eyes. I passed by him and entered the coffee shop. There were only a few people inside. I bought my treat and went to my usual place at the far back of the café to enjoy my moment. As I took off my coat, I saw the man in white standing right behind me very close, almost too close for New York standards. Behind him were two more men, also wearing white. I looked around and no one seemed to notice what was going on. I thought to myself, something does not add up here. I looked back again verifying that I was not daydreaming and they were still there. This is New York and anything can happen here, I said to myself. I sat down and the black man in white pulled up a chair on the other side of the table and said in the softest voice," We wish to speak with you, is that all right?"

My heart started to pump a bit faster. I thought maybe they wanted money but I said OK anyway, and then all of a sudden, I felt the noise around me quiet down. As if time stopped for a moment, and I could no longer hear the holiday music playing above me, nor the Spanish-speaking couple two tables down. The man said, "We want to speak to you about you and we wish you to take notes." Normally I would have said "… and *who* are you?" However looking at him, I felt as if I had to do what he said, as he emitted an energy that made me feel like melted butter. I pulled out my note book and pen, and without saying anything I waited. (I always carry my note book and pen in case some brilliant idea will cross my path. It is a habit from way back.) Somehow I felt that there was something so unusual about this that I had to just follow and flow with it. The man started to speak in a slow, soft tone. He had a low baritone voice. As he spoke, I felt so much love coming from him. The other two were right beside him sitting as well. I remember thinking that I did not see additional chairs at my table, and that it was strange. He spoke as a group and this is what he said: "We are angels like you and it is time we met. Please take notes." So I did.

The Buffet

I T IS OUR INTENTION TO LOVE YOU. *Why?*, you may ask. Because through the energy of love we communicate and connect to you, we are all linked through the invisible strings of love. *Why then is there not more of this love energy on this planet? Why is there so much anger and hate?*, you may wonder. It is because you must choose. The choice is always yours at any given moment. Although we give you love, it does not necessarily mean that you choose to accept it. The fact remains that we love you regardless of your choice. Whether you choose to use our love or ignore it, you are loved just the same. Doesn't this fact tell you something about spirit? Your learning is sacred. Your choices are sacred.

Where are we headed? you may ask. You are headed to where you choose to be. If we had to predict, we would say that you are headed to a higher place than ever before. We feel that your choices are such that you ascend continuously. *Why can't we feel it?*, you may ask. It is again your choice whether to feel it or not. You have a big table full of different kinds of food: from nutritious to junk, from divine taste to sour and spoiled. Some of you are used to sour and spoiled and may choose to eat it out of habit, some will choose to try the nutritious, and some will not touch the "good food" because they will not trust it. The food is available to you. The buffet-style table is full with an abundance of choices. The higher you vibrate, the more selection you will find. *How do you know what food is good and what will give you a bellyache?* you may ask. Your intent will lead you through your feeling centers. Spoiled food gives a foul smell; similarly, a bad choice emits a foul smell. Fresh, nutritious food offers a healthy, fresh, delicious smell. Your feeling center can be activated the same way as your sense of smell. As you choose to smell the food before you bite into it, you may choose to check in with your feeling center and sense how your choice smells. If it smells spoiled and you sense you will become sick after you eat it, why would you choose it?

We wish to explain that for each choice you make there is a color, a scent, a vibration, and energy. Just as a painter creates a picture based on the colors and brush strokes he chooses, so do you create the picture of your reality based on the ingredients you choose to mix. It is, however, a multidimensional picture and not a two-dimensional picture. The picture you may think you create in 2D looks very different when you go beyond 4D. Therefore, things are not always what they seem. More often than not it is quite the contrary. It is again the choice of the human to use the feeling center and go beyond the surface. Your emotions and your feelings are your biggest gifts, if you trust them and use them.

We have observed humanity for a long time. There was a time when your feeling centers were connected to the planet and you just "knew" what choice created what reactions. **You have, over millennia, moved away from your emotions and feelings, discarding them as feminine or irrational. You have moved away from the divine, feminine side of yourselves to the rational, masculine side. By doing so, you have created imbalance within yourselves and your relationships to the planet.** It is now, from our perspective, time for the pendulum to swing back. Some of you will choose to use the new tools available at this time to make new choices. These "new tools" will work better than ever because they are in line with the direction the pendulum is swinging. Those who will choose to disregard the new tools and make choices based on the old "rational tools" will find that the logic they were using is no longer working in the same linear fashion. In fact, many will find that 2+2 will equal 5. In such an environment, many of the assumptions that some of you will make will be proven wrong, and the results will be disappointing. Those, however, who choose to open up to how things feel rather than adding up the numbers, will find many doors open and more power to express, manifest, and stay balanced. **You**

are experiencing a shift of paradigm. This shift manifests on all levels of consciousness and therefore it is expressed through your biology as well. You are becoming more enabled than ever as a human. It is a wonderful time to smell the flowers, to slow down and "feel" your selves.

It is a time for celebration of your new potential, your new yous. *How would we celebrate?*, you may ask. We know who you are. Some of you have fears, doubts, anxiety, sickness, and everything seems to be going haywire. We are here to give you a hug and tell you that what you see is not what we see. We see you growing and learning to walk like a child who learns to use her legs to find balance. Of course, at times she falls and hurts her knees, maybe even bleeds a little. But this child we are seeing is determined to walk—and to walk by herself. We see a beautiful child on target to walk on her own soon. You may ask us, *how do you see that?* We see it because we can see your potential. The sums of your choices are heading toward that potential. Humanity is walking as if it had a compass and knows where North is. Learn to check within. Do not consult the newspapers, TV, or any other media for that matter. They will all tell you that things are gloomy. There is still a strong residue of fear-based economics, trades, and actions. Those modes, however, are weakening daily. Nevertheless, there are those who are still fighting to maintain their strong hold on your reality. They delay your shift in consciousness through fear. Fear blocks progress. Control blocks progress and creates fear. Understand that you are powerful—more powerful than you ever have been. You have the tools, and all you need to do is to choose. Every time you choose light over darkness you have tipped the balance and brought the shift that much closer. You do not need to be in politics or run for president to change this balance. You are who you are and who you are is just as loved as the next one. Each one makes a difference, and every new light that is ignited shows the way for many who are in the dark. The power of the one is immense. It is again inter-dimensional, where $1+1 = 100,000$. This is how powerful each and every one of you is who makes a choice every single day. And so be it.

A Car Without Fuel

WE ARE HERE TO SERVE. By serving you we are serving us. We are beings of light just like you. We come from various places in the universe. Some of us have been working with earth for a long, long time. We have always held special relationships to specific cultures. We were connected to the Egyptian mystery schools, to the Celts, to the Incas, the Mayan, the Tibetans, and to some indigenous tribes in Africa, South America, and North America. We look like you in the subtle form, but in physical form we are shape-shifters. We can be what we wish to be. We can appear in the form of an animal, a flower, a cloud, a human, or the wind. We are masters of energy transcendence. It is merely a small shift for us to turn from a human to a rock or from a tree to a frog. This is merely a physical ability that we hold, and it is talked about in your mythology.

Our true essence is love, and your true essence is love. That is why we are calling ourselves your brothers and sisters. You are connected to us in so many ways, and your future is our present. Your destiny will not only affect you but us as well.

There is much we wish to share with you as our brothers and sisters. We want to hold you and let you know that you are loved. We want to tell you to trust the process and accept the fact that you are much greater then the sum of your parts. We wish to tell you that your journey is about remembering who you really are. The experiences that you are now living through are merely awakening bells aimed to bring you out of a deep sleep. You have been asleep, and now the alarm clock is ringing. The ring gets stronger over time, so even those who are deep sleepers or hearing-impaired will wake up eventually.

There is no judgment in the order in which you are awakened. It is a fact, however, that those who are awakened will find it simpler and more joyful to experience the moment-by-moment stream of events that will pass in front of them.

In the vast space you call your universe, there are many who are concerned with your well-being. There are multitudes of energies from all over who come to your assistance. You are never alone. There is nothing you do that we are not aware of. There is nothing you do that the universe as you call it is not aware of. You are like a giant elephant in a small zoo. Your energy is large, and it is just natural that your action will be noticed and measured. Although there are many of you, there are many more of us. When you are not walking on the physical planet, you are one of us. You chose your experience on planet Earth because you knew you were needed. We promised you to look after you from this side of things. We are, in fact, on the same side, but to you that "other side" does not exist because you cannot observe it with your senses. We are here to tell you that many of you will soon be able to see the other side while walking in your physical bodies on earth. It is an attribute that is now being developed, encouraged, and enabled. Your path will look very different from the standpoint of spirit. It is grand, grand beyond your wildest imagination. While you are working the grind of day-to-day challenges, insecurities, struggles, and pains, you are also moving through these challenges to places where there is peace, balance, beauty, and love. More and more of you are finding the place we call "home" while walking inside your skin. Your planet is like a large-size scale that is measuring the ones who are with the light and the ones who are without. Those ones of the light carry much more weight, so the few of you can tip the scale for the whole of humanity. The planet is the scale. It is connected to the energy that you are emitting. As you emit and exude, so the energy changes. So, the few of you are doing the work for the multitudes. We do not see that you will receive medals of honor and red-carpet treatments from your establishments. As unlikely as that, you will be honored in ways beyond your imagination on the other side. You will also be showered with gifts of enablement, peace, balance, and health while living out your daily lives. This is our promise to you.

It is your desire that fuels the engine of reality in your dimensions. Those who tell you what to feel want to funnel your desires to a place where they can benefit from it. Your desires are the diamond jewels of your dimensions. It is the energy of creation that moves the molecules around you and changes matter. Your desires can be created based on the choices you make. If you aim your desires at "things," your return, however limited in scope, will materialize as things. If you aim your desires towards peace, balance, and abundance, it is the reality that will manifest in front of you. Your desires are your power as your passion is your vehicle to move from one place to another. **When you do what you deeply desire and are passionate about it, the energy you transmit is powerful. When you choose to do something that is a "compromise" in order to meet your responsibilities and make ends meet, it is as if you were, from our perspective, attempting to drive a fast new car without fuel. You are pushing the car with your hands or legs while trying to move forward.** The actual ingredient that propels the car forward is put aside. **If you were wondering why many of you who "act responsibly" and "do the right thing" for the benefit of your families or communities feel so depressed and joyless, then understand that without passion your actions do not carry the joy that you know you can feel.** It is through the energy that you

create while doing the things that fulfill you the most, that you make music.

You have been sidetracked by many modern-day desires of things. It is no wonder to us that many of you feel empty although you have all the material comfort you could wish for. Many of you buy in to what you have been told: "Drive this beautiful car, and you will be happy." It looks funny from where we stand. You can see a very dim light pushing a brand new fancy car uphill without actually using the engine. At the same time, we see some of you who shine so brightly that you need no car at all. You can be anywhere you wish to be on time without ever having to deal with traffic. This is what it looks like from here. And you wonder why we love you so much. It is your not-knowing that makes your "reality" so compelling to us. If you would see what we see, there would be no need to choose. Choosing wouldn't even be a question. It is the part of your test. You are here at this time because you know that you have the choice to "see" and figure out this puzzle, changing the actual fabric of the universe. What greater honor can one sign on for? When you find your true passion, there is no power in the world that can hold you back. You will have to face tests and challenges, but you will propel forward no matter what obstacles you will encounter. If your passion has been bought or borrowed from others or the media, your progress will be slow and, from our perspective, "joyless."

Again, it is your choice and we are here to honor your journey. Honor yourself, honor earth and life, and know that you are never alone. It is why you came here. And so we wish you hello, and so be it.

Small Holding Cell

WE WANT TO THANK YOU for doing what it is that you are doing. *What is it that I am doing?* you may ask. You are bridging the universal energy, bringing it through your own vessel and sending it to those places in need. *How does it happen?* you may ask. It is a process that happens automatically once you have mastered two obstacles: removing ego and surrendering, moving your self to the side. *How do I know that what I am experiencing is real?* you may ask. What is real in your dimension is not necessarily real in ours. What you see is, again, not what we see. You only experience what is in front of your nose—those things you can smell touch, feel, hear, or see. We see the circle that transcends time and space. We see the sum of your choices and where it leads in the sense of an outcome. We see that one person being touched may reverberate to many people over a period of time. We see that this one person who changed may inspire his or her spouse, his or her children and friends and, thus, creating an ever-growing circle of energy that expands beyond your ability to perceive from where you are standing. We may ask you a question, if that is okay. How do you feel when you do what you do; sitting in front of a candle sending light? How does your body feel? How do your hands and spine feel? Do you feel different? Are you calmer? Are you more peaceful? Does your body feel whole? These are your markers. Are certain people attracted to you because they have something to learn? At times you will not even need to interact with them. They will absorb your energy and shift. You will not know their names, and they will not know yours. This is how it works. The energy is quiet, it is invisible, and yet it connects all of you and us and, for that matter, the rest of the universe.

There is a paradox in the existence on your planet. Those things that matter the most are invisible, cannot be claimed, and cannot be capitalized. It is built that way. It is part of the design. Everyone wants to become rich because your culture promotes the idea that wealth makes one more powerful and leads to a better life. This is an illusion, of course. If spiritual progress is measured by external wealth, everyone would obviously try to attain it in any way they could. It would be clear that "as you accumulate, so your happiness grows." Such a design, in our view, would not be a test. It would be clear to all that $1+1=2$. Spirit wished to create a test that transcends the limited scope in which you perceive your reality. Your spiritual growth had to be in some way counterintuitive, invisible, and subtle. It had to be discovered from within and not from the outside and it had to be voided of ego. It had to be like spirit. That made the test real, and your choices more difficult.

It is our intention to help you realize your full potential by guiding you through the mechanism of spirit. From our perspective it is simple. You have two main tools and the rest is a variation on this theme. The first is love, and the second is intent. These two are the vehicle and the fuel. For us, it seems clear because we are on the spirit side of the veil. This is not your reality, however. You are so dearly loved because you choose to test yourself under conditions of blindness, deafness, and limitation. Your goal has been to discover spirit within, without any of the tools you possess when you are on the other side. Now that is courage. Your journey is greatly honored. *How do I know that this is real?* you may ask. You will know if you use the tools of love and intent. Knowing comes from feeling. It is the feeling that defines who you are. Your emotions define your reality. When you know something through your feeling centers and your emotions that is your "real" truth.

It is by design that you have been programmed not to trust your feelings. There are those who operate in the shadow of darkness who wish to harness your emotional energy. This is very valuable to them. Like you, they use it as energy to propel themselves. You have been diverted to

move away from your emotions, to doubt your emotions, to control your emotions, and to learn to re-direct your emotions. These are all campaigns of manipulation to steer you away from your truth. You have been taught that possessing certain items that you can see and hold in your hand, wear on you, or drive are real and, therefore, will make your life more rewarding. Your emotions have been programmed to direct energy away from the inside and toward the outside. From our perspective, this notion does not achieve the results you have been sold on. But clearly, the programming, habits, and social pressures are strong, and when you feel empty and depressed despite all these things you have achieved, you are sold medication to numb you even further, or you are sent to a psychologist who teaches you coping techniques. Trusting your emotions and following your feelings are where the ultimate truth lies. When you trust your emotions, you are free; you do not need a logo or a brand to know who you are. That knowing makes you powerful and makes those who want to sell you things weaker. The universe is also designed that way. From our perspective it is beautiful that you can choose. Choice is powerful. It is something you appreciate in your governments and democracies. It is something you fought for throughout your history. You know intuitively that you are free. It is strange to us that many of you willingly subscribe to small holding cells and lock yourselves in front of your HD TV. Your TV is the modern answer to a holding cell. It communicates a message that re-programs your perception, which tells you what is "normal" and what you are "supposed" to feel, how you are supposed to behave. It communicates the message that unless you saw or heard it on TV, it is not real or true. It tells you how you are supposed to dress and look as well as what is considered attractive and whom you should admire or despise. You are being sold twenty-four hours a day products that limit your ability to fly. Given you have the choice of channels and programming, we are not here to tell you that all the programs on TV are such. It is as if you travel to a new exotic island, a place you always wanted to go to because everyone was raving how beautiful it is, and when you finally get there, you choose to stay in your hotel room and look at the picture book someone else left for you so you can "experience" the island. When you finally finish your vacation and return, your "adventures" will consist of the pictures and descriptions you read in your hotel room.

We honor your choices, and there is no judgment. You are a divine being. You are like us: You are light. We love you and connect to you in more ways than you can ever imagine. We wish you to grow, expand, wake up, explore, and experience joy, health, and abundance. It is with a hug that we say goodbye to you. We are never too far. And so be it.

Earth's Sister Planet

I T I S O U R I N T E N T I O N to allow infinite growth. From our perspective, you are unlimited in your capabilities to create. It is you who create your own limits by adopting certain beliefs. We wish to tell you that you have no beginning and no end. You have always been and always will be. The past, present, and future are combined in our reality. It is one continuum that stretches onto itself. All possibilities are available for us to see. As you limit yourself to a linear continuum, it appears to you that one event follows the other. In fact, all events are planned simultaneously. It is only your intention and choice that navigate through the infinite possibilities.

There are many forces that operate in the universe. The universe teems with life. You are a combination of various forms of intelligent life. You have seeds sprouted from different systems to allow you to be in this reality. Some of your capabilities have been limited and locked, and some are re-enabled. When you and we join together, we are made of the same energetic substance. We have our own journey. It is a journey that includes supporting you in a manner that allows your free choice. Whatever you see, hear, taste, smell, and touch does not hold the same energy that it used to. It can no longer be trusted in the same way. Your senses, at this time, are your detractors. It is your challenge at this time to develop your "other" senses, those you once possessed and lost. In the time of the mystery schools, initiates used to be deprived of any sense so they could develop their clairvoyant abilities. At this time it is not necessary. You are enabled.

Many of the visions that you will witness are illusions designed to limit your capacity to move more deeply. When you agree to accept the version of reality you are being offered, it is as if you willingly agree to be blindfolded right when you pass by the most breathtaking views. **There are many who wish to block your vision. They spend vast resources to create an environment that diverts you from the true picture. This environment is embedded with frequencies of fear that hold you like an anchor in the harbor so you cannot sail to the open sea.** If you teach yourself to smell this frequency, you will discover that it does not smell good. One way of moving away from this "trap" is by closing your eyes and turning off whatever device you use to feed yourself with information. Touch your heart with your left hand and your third eye with your right. Breathe deeply and slowly for two to three minutes. This simple gesture allows your heart enough time to decipher the information and form a feeling. You will have access to the truth, and then you will need to choose which version of it to accept. We will ask you to choose the latter one. It is a simple method, but can be powerful when used often and with intent to move beyond your current state of awareness.

Knowing is your most empowering state of awareness. Knowing comes from feeling. For you to develop this sense, you must learn to bring your awareness to that part of the body that holds the feeling. Through this awareness, you learn to acknowledge and process that sense. As you become more proficient and sensitive, you will know how to qualify events when you experience them. You will then be empowered to know truth from illusion. You will have gained the knowing. The events will register in your body without being tainted by prejudices. The ability to think and to use logic can be an obstacle when you grow spiritually and become more interdimensional. Your feeling center, though, bypasses your processing mind and reaches your knowing, which does not need explanation or justification. It is the knowing of "I am that I am."

There is a place in the universe similar to yours. You can call it your sister planet. It is set up in a similar fashion to earth. It has trees and animals, oxygen and nitrogen. This planet also contains intelligent life. Unlike yours, there are no people walking around. Call it an "experimental lab planet" whose work is designing the very same evolutionary path that you are now experiencing. When you are not here, you are also designing your own experiments on this planet. It is with great care that these experiments are conducted there. This planet is hidden from you although you are connected to it energetically. The human race as it appears now in its "modern" version was first developed on this sister planet. Why are we telling you this? Because the path you are pursuing was designed by you for your benefit. You are the designer as well as the executioner. It is you who chose to experience the tests that you are experiencing. As you struggle with the idea of "intelligent design," we find it ironic that indeed it is the same intelligence that occupies your biology that designed those same things you are now struggling to define and understand.

This planet holds the "pure version" of its sister planet, which is planet Earth. The energy between those two planets can be compared to the connection between identical twins. Even more so. It is the energetic exchange between the planets that enables earth to remain balanced. It is all about balance. This version of earth holds the original intention for your earth. It is the paradise that you strive for. It is the image that you keep seeing in your mythology. It is the pure earth that all of you have seen when not in a body. You still hold that memory, and you always will. The "lab," as we like to call it, is your favorite playground. It holds the ideal balance of spirit consciousness, male-female energies. There, you experiment with the highest potential for your future.

You also know that if your planet dies, the "lab earth" or "paradise" dies as well. They are connected with the same umbilical cord although physically far apart. Whatever you do on your earth registers in "real time" on the sister earth. The sister planet energetically holds your non-dual self, the part connected to spirit. It is through love that we maintain the energy on the sister planet. It is through love that you heal your earth. You are on a brink of an astonishing leap. It is why we love you so. And so be it.

A Farmer in Northern China

WE WISH TO EXPLORE the relationship you have with yourself and others. Those relationships are comprised of, as we see it, layers of energy patterns. Each pattern has its own signature. You are a nucleus of bundled energy. The way you "see" yourself and others emits the frequency that comprises the way you "appear" to us. We "see" you not as one entity walking within a skin, but more of an energy pattern comprised of certain hues, sounds, and vibrations. **From where we stand, who you are has nothing to do with what you do, how much you have, or your social status.** You can be the president of a corporation, the head of a political group, or a farmer in Northern China who still plows his field using an ox. Your "appearance," from our vantage point, has little to do with any of the items that you, as a human, use to judge your fellow human. **We do not distinguish between rich and poor, nor do we relate differently to those who have more social influence, political power, or outer beauty. From the side we are standing on, these are external roles you came to play in order to grow and learn.** They are temporary, fleeting experiences that enrich your "earthly" journey and prompt you to grow and define who you are in relationship to your own self and those around you. Those relationships are actually one and the same. The way you are seeing yourself extends to the way you see others. It is a continuum. This is why we ask you to love yourself first. No love for others can be powerful, genuine, or transformative unless you first learn to love yourself.

All your experiences while on earth have a primary learning and a secondary learning. Your primary learning will always involve learning to love yourself. It is the primary, essential choice you are asked to make through your duality. It is the cord that connects you with your higher you and with spirit. It is the "secret" you came to discover: your own divinity, your own transcendent nature. All of the closed doors will open and reveal your true nature if you use the key of "self-love." As you love and honor yourself, you will naturally extend that honor and love to your fellow humans, to the plants and animals that are here to support you on your journey, and to planet Earth.

Lifetime after lifetime, you have chosen different roles to play. In all of these roles you have had to experience the cycle of birth and death. In birth, you come equipped for self-love. Through your own chosen path, that initial self-love will be challenged and tested. This testing is the reason you came here. This fact is true for all of you, not just those who are weak or poor or sick. The tests you will encounter were designed by you and others to prompt you to higher planes. **From where we stand, there are no arbitrary lessons. All your experiences are planned and executed perfectly for your learning.** From the perspective of 4D, it is difficult to conceive the larger picture. As you walk in your daily life, doing what you are doing, you are shielded from the wider inter-dimensional purpose of it all. To many of you, experiences come at times as great surprises, positive and negative. As we walk beside you and hold your hand in love, we see the pain and victimhood outfit you put on when things do not work the way you expected. We want to assure you that whatever your experiences, know that you have designed it for yourself. Your lessons are by choice, your choice. You may say to us that you would have never designed a lesson in which you have to face losing a loved one, experiencing pain and suffering. We are here to tell you that we love you, and those whom you loved and lost participated with you in the planning. It is the part of you that is not with you, your higher self, who is involved with the planning.

It is on you to become peaceful and loving despite the experiences you encounter. You have evolved and changed throughout your earthly cycles. During your many cycles you have collected certain energies that need to be balanced. It is all about balance. There is never a judgment.

This energy is called karma. Karma has a weight. It is something that you carry as you move from lesson to lesson. Your colors, sounds, and vibrations tell us the story of your lives. They tell us about your lessons. When we see the colors of self-love, there is usually a very light load as the load of karma has been cleared along the way. Self-love acts as a "repellant" for new karma so that things do not "stick" as easily.

When you love yourself, you assume the energy of balance; therefore, imbalance does not affect you, and it is absorbed in your balance. Those who emit the colors of self-love are the ones who emit the most brilliant radiant energy around them. Your mission at this time, as we see it, is to be the one to discover the "I am" and to be in love with yourself.

When we see those who act against the energy of self-love on behalf of God, we find it ironic. You have been searching for God throughout history, often forcing your fellow humans to love the God that you love. We wish to hold your hands with love and tell you that all along God was waiting patiently inside of you to be discovered. Discovering spirit is the greatest choice a human can make, and the inability to recognize this fact is why we observe so much misunderstanding in that search.

Now is a time of change. You are coming near the end of your lesson. Many of you carry the colors of balance. Some of you may ask, *how come the world seems to be more chaotic now than ever?* We are here to tell you that it is part of the lesson. It is on you to find the truth hidden behind the veil of chaos. Use your feeling, find the balance in you. You are shifting on many dimensions at once. Time is accelerating and the magnetic fields around you are changing. Your biology is changing as well. You are more equipped than ever before to love yourself, to *be* balance, and to use the "key" of love to solve the challenges that face you. And we love you so, and so be it.

The Movie Theater

SHALL WE BEGIN? During the course of a day, you may experience fluctuations of emotions, which can vary from elation to despair, from joy to sadness. It requires very little, from our perspective, for you to move yourselves from one point of the scale to the other. You are easily manipulated and are able to express the gamut of emotions within one breath. *So what?*, you may ask. We have told you that your emotions are energy. We also told you that there are those who benefit from a certain emotional range that is known as fear. There are still those who harvest those energies known to you as anger. It is the emotional ability you possess that so many in the universe are after. You are unique in that regard.

Your emotional scale carries the seed of spirit. It is powerful. When your emotions are in line with the energy of spirit, it travels to the far reaches of the universe instantaneously. You may encounter events in your day-to-day life that can make you feel like the light, white ball in a ping-pong game. It is the illusion we wish to tell you about: You are using much of your energies to feed darkness rather than the light. If you are watching a movie, which may include happy scenes and sad scenes, in the back of your mind you know that the movie's story is an illusion created for your entertainment, education, or enjoyment. You know that when you step out of the theater you will be waving goodbye to the movie and returning to your "real life." You have chosen to pay money, stand in line, and sit through the movie in return for you gaining an experience.

You have access to whatever experience you choose as there is a large selection to choose from. We wish to tell you that from where we stand looking at you, it is a movie that you are experiencing in your "real life." That is why we love you so. It is because you choose to be shielded from the fact that you are sitting in a theater. You were blocked from having our seats. **We want you to know that those daily life scenes you were crying on or laughing at and those scenes that made you cringe or smile are events produced for you in the world of "spirit-Hollywood" so you can grow spiritually and evolve.**

I can feel the pain; this is for real, you may say. The movie that you are in is multi-sensory, and, yes, it includes all your senses. It is only by quieting all the senses that you can experience reality. *Why then am I here?* , you may ask. *Why am I going through all this just to learn how to quiet all this stimulation?* This is your test. We want to remind you that you designed it in such a way that you can pass it with flying colors every time. There is not a single human on earth who came to this life bound to fail his or her test. We wish to help you pass your own test. You can call us the tutors of light. We wish you to succeed. Like a test in school, there are trick answers made to steer you away from the correct answer. These distracting options may seem similar and even logical, but they will still give you the wrong answer. You know that 2+2=4. If you answer 5, it is close, but is it a false answer.

As you breach your current level of consciousness and ascend in your vibration, you are generating more light. There are those who feed on darkness. They wish you to generate the kind of emotions they can use. They do it by tipping the scale oh-so-lightly to move your response from one end of the scale to the other. They are masters of illusions, and they perfected their moviemaking techniques to such a level of mastery that most of you believe it is reality you are experiencing. You are the master. It is your test. You paid for it. You purchased the ticket to watch the movie of your choice. You are part of spirit. Your essence is love. You have come to experience an environment of free choice, one in which spirit is hiding inside of you, and you need to discover it one action at a time, one emotion at a time. **By discovering the light within you, you pass the test, you change everything. We wish to tell you that your feelings are your tools. Use them**

appropriately and you will have access to the most powerful treasure on earth: you.

What will I gain by quieting my senses?, you may ask. When you try to speak with someone during a rock concert, you may lose the subtleties of the conversation. Spirit communicates with you all the time. You are linked. It is through finding a quiet space in which no outside noises overshadow the message that you can gain insight to the message being conveyed. When you are immersed in a deafening noise, the message of spirit likely will not come through.

Why do I need this message?, you may ask. Love, joy, compassion, happiness, balance, harmony, health, and beauty are the experiences you asked for. At times those are shielded by despair, anxiety, anger, depression, and sickness. You may have chosen to take the movie you paid for too seriously and be too affected by it. You believed in it and became one of the characters. Instead of using it as a tool for growth, you became its victim. Do you like being schemed? Manipulated? Angry or depressed? We would like to hold you by the hand for just one moment and carry you out of the movie theater. We wish to show you that it is only a movie. We wish to give you the comfort of "home" where there is only love and light, and where no duality exists. We promise that after this "intermission" from the movie, as you go back to your seat and watch it until the end, whatever your experience may be, in the back of your mind you will remember the feeling of your true home. You will know inside that it is only a movie made for your entertainment, so you will be more committed to be entertained. You may also decide that this movie is not for you and walk out only to become a director of a new movie. As director, you possess the tools to create the new "movie" that you wish to see, the one with the happy ending.

Like tutors who provide their students with a technique to pass an exam, we only wish to give you tools so that you may choose the correct answer for you. It is a special time for you. It is the test season on planet Earth. Light is coming in, and it becomes stronger by the day. Your light, the one generated from the energy of your actions and thought, is growing. Those who feed on emotions of fear and anger are threatened by this new light. It is light that transforms darkness, and not the opposite. Light is active. However, those of darkness will create many movies to try and manipulate your emotions so they can continue their feeding frenzy. If you remember that it is up to you to choose whichever movie fits you, and that it is only a movie, you will stay with the energy of light, love, joy, and balance regardless of the movie's content.

This is our message for today. We hold your hand all the time. We feel you all the time. We walk beside you all the time. You are never alone. You are always loved. To feel our hands you need to find a quiet spot. It is in the absence of stimulation that you may experience us, because we are subtle, like you. You have taken a body, and we did not. When you go home, you are with us, and we are just like brothers and sisters, and so be it.

The Different "Yous"

WHAT IS IT THAT MAKES YOU DIFFERENT than your fellow humans? Are we at all different? What is the common thread that connects all of us? What separates us? We are a group, but we speak to you as one. We speak in one voice. That is the way of spirit.

You, like us, are also a group. You may think that because your body is contained within skin you are singular, but in actuality you too have different "yous" that play a role in your singular appearance.

You are contained in a vessel whose sole purpose is to express the will of the group. *I do not feel like a group*, you may say. *I do not see anyone around me. I feel alone.* Have you ever had a conversation with yourself? Did you ever try to convince yourself? Do you ever talk with yourself, out loud or in your head? Whom do you think you were talking to? The group that is you is conversing twenty-four hours a day. They are made of trillions of yous that are your cells. It is the you behind the veil, hidden from your limited self that is on the other side, working together and planning the next step or shall we call it the "now" step. Those two are also in communication with your cells telling them of your intents. Your cells as you know are never asleep. When you are asleep, they are working on balancing your biology, fighting bacteria, metabolizing and ingesting the food, sending oxygen to the blood and to the brain, pumping your heart.

Each of the cells that make up what you call you has consciousness. Each one listens to you and works with you. They don't argue or rebel, and they are aware of you who give the instruction. Don't you think the cells in your lungs can distinguish between fresh air or smoke and tar? When you eat processed food, do you think the cells that metabolize the food are not aware of your choices? Each of your cells is like a soldier in a disciplined army. Your cells work in unison. They do what they need to do so your vessel will function optimally. They are part of spirit, and they have the light encoded within the cell structure. **As you walk in your body contemplating life and going through your day, you have an enormous support group. You have your cells, your higher selves, and then there are others. You may call them angels or guides. They are part of you, yet separated. They are the link between you and your higher you. They also translate some of the messages from your cells, injecting thoughts into you so you may consider alternatives.** They are always respectful and honor your wishes. These angels are with you in your lightest moments and in your darkest as well. Those energies walk with you waiting for the moment that you will ask them to help you. They are the ones who whisper in your dreams the answer to a problem that has been bothering you. They are your aid, your facilitators, your guides, and they love you.

The common thread between all of the different "yous" is that they all listen to you. This is the same with your higher self and your cells. The one who is "you," walking on earth in a linear singular reality is the one who makes the ultimate decision for the group. It is not because this "you" is the smartest or the most enlightened. It is the "you" who volunteered to participate in the play, taking the role to discover the real "you" hidden within you. When you signed up for the role, a contract was signed. All of the "yous" were there to sign. The contract read that within the sacred mission of coming to earth and living the cycle you call life, your wishes will be honored regardless if they are respectful to your biology, life, or Gaia. Your choices will be honored and respected without judgment. The contract also read that you will be held at all times and guided at all times and that the love link between you and spirit will be maintained regardless of the choices you make. In fact, the contract reads that you are never alone and you are always loved.

Why are you telling this to us?, you may ask. *We feel singular, and we act as singular, so what difference does it make?* It is our understanding that when you learn to listen to your other "yous" in the group, then you may experience the cycle you call life in its highest form. From where we stand, we wish you to take the best advice so you can experience your life to the fullest. It is through understanding who you are and allowing those parts of you to show you the path that the "marriage" of biology and spirit occurs. Only when you learn to listen to your cells, your higher self and your guides and angels, will you experience the full joy of spirit within your biology. It is that marriage that changes your biology and changes this planet and beyond. The journey of discovery is to live your life being aware of your group. Your life becomes inter-dimensional, and you walk hand-in-hand with the greatest masters who ever walked on this planet. You become the true master. Through surrendering your limited linear idea of who you are, the other "yous" emerge.

Your modern science tells you that one human is not very different than the other. In fact, your modern-day genealogy shows that many of you come from the same ancestors. From our perspective you are all on the same track of learning. Some of you have been experiencing Earth life cycles many more times than others, and the lessons and learning are therefore different. However, all of you have the same route to walk and the same exams to pass. You are together in the grandest school of all, the school of free choice. No two of you have the exact same learning, but you all agreed to help each other at this time to graduate and complete your degrees with honors. All of you stood in line to come to earth at this time, because you knew that this was the "place to be." You knew that there was no greater honor than to discover the hidden and to transform the heavy to light, illness to health, and dark to light. You signed up for this mission, all of you. You all have the same purpose.

So why are we so different?, you ask. **You are not different at all. You are like us, an angelic energy whose purpose is to become one through creation.** Your oneness is hidden from you, but as more light floods your planet, those outer layers that have camouflaged your oneness are being peeled away, and you begin to feel your oneness. It is an awesome power to realize your oneness and to set an intention to vibrate at a higher frequency. Discovering your true purpose and your oneness will manifest a bridge of light that will open the path to a new consciousness. And so be it.

The Magic Manual

IT IS A GAME. You are a player. Like any game, sometimes you "win," and sometimes you "lose." However, it is only a game. There are rules to the game. If you choose to violate the rules, you pay fines. The rules are not your human-made rules. We refer to the cosmic or universal rules. The point that we are making is that it is a game. As we see it, it is a grand game, indeed. Those of you who have played the game many times and accumulated experience naturally will be more adept and savvy in some ways.

We are the observers of the game. We are the audience, you might say. You are the players. We are your admirers, fans, and supporters. We wish all of you to win. The interesting thing about the game you are playing is that there is only one group. And each player is playing against himself. The game is played by the individual within. The winner is declared when enough of you players win against yourselves. We see you as a point of light. When one is winning, she or he is transmitting more light. The brighter the light, the better the individual is doing. The dimmer the light, the more difficult is the inner struggle. There is no light when the individual stops playing and gives up the game.

With every game arrives a manual of sorts. The original manuals have been tampered with; so you, at this time, must find the original manual stored within your cells. To access this manual, all you need to do is ask for it with pure intention, and it will be given to you.

We want to let you know that this manual is somewhat different than those you get with your technology. When you get a gadget, you usually have to open the box, read the manual, and start operating the device. This set of instructions is different. As you walk in your daily life, you carry this manual within your cells, inside your body. In essence, it is you who walks hand-in-hand with the manual. As you approach an intersection, deciding whether to turn left or right, the manual will open to you and will instruct you to the right direction. You do not need to know in advance which direction you will need to turn. Moreover, even if you want to be more diligent and read the manual overnight to prepare for the next day, the manual will not be available. It will be blank. It is a "tricky" manual in a sense that it is different than the one you used in the past. This one has no predetermined way of doing things. It has a built-in GPS system that tracks you at any given moment. It knows where you are and what is it that you are doing. The set of instructions are continuously being updated. It is indeed a magical manual.

That does not sound right, you may say. *How can we plan? We need to know how to prepare for what is to come.*

We love you so, and that is why we are here to tell you that the format of the manual has changed. You have changed it. Your reality has changed, time as you know it has changed, and your magnetic fields are changing. The former set of instructions is no longer correct or up-to-date. If you try to follow it, you may get lost. Your new compass and GPS system work with your biology. Each and every one of you is enabled to use this new manual. You do need to learn how to use it, however. Like any new skill, using this manual requires some adapting, and you may make some mistakes. The first step in learning this new manual is to acknowledge it, and the second step is to set an intention to learn how to use it. The third step is to follow what it tells you and not to doubt it. It is simple. It is 1, 2, 3, and off you go. However, like an infant who learns to walk, you may tell the infant that it is simple, that all she needs to do is put one leg in front of the other, a two-step, or even one-step learning process, but we all know that walking sounds simpler than it is. She must use the skill of balance, perseverance, trial and error, scaffolding, and the wall.

There are some of us who wish to read you the instructions

as you walk and act. We wish to hold your hands, and we do. But it is you who must want to learn the new skills. It is you who needs to ask for our guidance. There is a universal law on this planet: free choice. Your choice is honored without judgment. If you wish to use the manual, you will find that your life becomes easier, more joyous, and more balanced.

How do we know that what we are getting is the truth? Maybe we tell ourselves that we need to turn right because we want it? Maybe the instructions will come from us and not from the manual? How do we know? It is your intention that will set you down the correct path. If your intention is to fool yourself, you will indeed do that. You are a master in disguise. You can pretend to be a human, a victim, or the one who is led by circumstances. It is funny to us that as kings and queens you always like to play dress up as subjects and beggars. It is indeed your choice, and we honor you for whatever choices you may select. We are here to show you that you are the master of your own destiny, and by using the manual inside of you, you are enabled to never go on the wrong path.

Why is it that so many of us do go on the wrong path? How come no one heard of this "magic manual"?, you may ask. If you listen to the news, it will tell you of those who are not guided by this "magic manual." We are here to tell you that many of you do follow it. You do not hear about them on TV, radio, and your newspapers as much as you hear about the others. Still, there are many around you, and many more are joining them daily. *How do we know that this is correct?*, you ask. How does a child know that he or she can walk? They do not, but they feel that they can. It is built in them, and they do not fear the trying. Be like an infant, and learn to walk. Remind yourself that it is built inside of you, and soon this memory will surface. You will no longer need a set of instructions to know right from wrong. You will become a sacred set of instructions yourself. It is then that the memory of your enablement will come back to you, and you will wonder how you managed before.

Everything that we speak of, you already know. You know deep inside that you are the kings and queens; more so, you know that you are the creators of your own destiny. You also know that you are angels, walking in plain clothes, pretending to be humans. We are here to hug you and to remind you of your divinity, of your power and of your inner beauty. We want to hold you all the time and to just tell you that you are loved. We see you in your struggles, we see you in your pain, and we see you all the time as we are with you all the time. When you call for us, we are already there. We never leave you, not even for a moment. So next time instead of calling us, just give yourself a hug and then congratulate yourself for knowing that you are loved for who you are. When you do that, you will feel us joining the hug as well. You will feel our warmth, our scent, and maybe even a faint melody. It is us, and we are here with you.

You are our brothers and sisters. We have been with you forever, and we will always be with you. For us, a lifetime is a second, and a second is a lifetime. Time is your game. Our game is love. And so we say goodbye, but we actually never leave. And so be it.

The Air that You Breathe

SOMEWHERE IN THE UNIVERSE are those whose purpose is to link you with yourself. It is a sacred link. Only when you are disconnected from yourself does your body become useless and your soul return home. They are facilitators of the transition you call death.

We love you. We know that death causes fear in you. You are built that way. If you knew what we know, you would go back home without resistance. In fact, it would be just a simple step for you that would require neither effort nor hesitation. **You are built to fight for life and to fear death. You are built for survival. It is ironic to us that many of you are in survival mode, trying so hard to stay alive, and at the same time you do not honor the life of others and of earth.** Many on earth at this time have yet to link the life of the planet to their life. If the physical planet dies, all its inhabitants die as well. The life of the planet is dependent on the life of humanity, and the life of humanity is dependent on the planet. One cannot survive without the other. This relationship is intermingled in many different ways. Earth and you are one. When we say that

Gaia has consciousness and it is alive, it is through its relationship with you. You are at a place where the curtain of forgetfulness thins and more of you remember who you are and your purpose. Some of you choose also to make the transition home because you remember that it is just a change of energy and you can be more useful on the other side of things. There is no judgment if you choose to come back. You are loved just the same.

The energy that links you to yourself is like a silver string connected energetically to each cell of your body. Your cells are the ones that communicate with the other side. It is your mind that then must interpret the signs coming from your cells. Some of you consider the brain to be the center of the higher self or spiritual knowledge. From our understanding, it is each and every cell of your body that communicates messages back and forth to the energy remaining on the other side.

Why leave any energy on the other side at all?, you may ask. The energy left is your home, your center. It is the part of you that is linked to spirit, and it does all the planning behind the scenes. Like a play on stage, there is much planning and preparation needed to be done so the play will be presented cohesively and successfully. The energy left behind is responsible to communicate with all the other energies so the planning will be executed perfectly. In fact, if you combine the processing power of all the computers now on earth, it would still be insufficient to plan a single human's life walking the earth. An awesome processing of energy through this silver line is occurring.

The facilitators of transition are very special light beings, and we would like to introduce them to you so you will not fear them. They are actually those who say *goodbye* to you when you descend to the dimension of earth and enter the fetus, and they are the ones who say *hello* to you when you are leaving your body and return home. Their energy is with you all the time as they maintain the connection. They have great responsibility and are competent. Their essence is of love like yours. They, however, do not incarnate. They do not have an earth experience or any physical experience. Part of their responsibility is to assist your energy transmission with as little trauma to the body as possible. It requires a great skill, however, not to facilitate this transition too soon, so the experience of your cycle on earth will be complete. The entering and exiting to and from the physical plane is important, like the first scene of a play and the last scene of a play. In those scenes, you are being imprinted with your lessons, your realization, and your karma. It does happen at times that the transition facilitator will pull the energy too soon. Some of you have experienced and reported it as "near-death experience." It is our understanding that the experiences of those who seemingly died and came back to life, and therefore reported it, is that they did not die.

The "death" transition is different energetically and experientially. Those whose energy may have been pulled "too soon" and later returned have experienced what we may call expanded awareness and were able to sense the actual connection that you have everyday of your life with the other side. Their experience is closer to what we may consider your "real" reality. *How come we do not see these things?*, you may ask. We do not see our dead parents or our best friends who passed. We do not see light beings who transmit so much love and deliver us beautiful messages. We wish to tell you: Yes, you do have the capability and access to the same experience while walking in a physical body on earth at this time. You do not need to "nearly die" to experience it. If anything, you need to begin to live more fully. *How do we do that?*, you may ask. *We tried everything.* It is not in the trying, but in the letting go of trying and just learning to be where this experience lies. It is in the spaces between the actions that the treasure lies.

We wish to tell you that, indeed, you are surrounded by your loved ones. Their energy is actually part of your aura. You also have loving light beings with you all the time and they hold your hand. They are your guides or angels. Some people have reported that they have felt much love emanating from these angels who appeared from the light. These guides are available to you 24/7. They are with you all the time, and when you connect to them at any given moment you will feel this love energy. This love energy never fluctuates; it is always available for you to access. You, however, must choose it and wish to connect to it.

Some of you relate this connection to God. You talk about this God and that God, and some of you make a whole ritual around connecting to this love energy. Some of you even coerce and force others to connect to this source. Throughout history, much blood has been shed to transfer this love energy from one to another. It is again an irony to us that you need to build institutions, create structures, pay money, and coerce other humans for connecting to something that is with each of you all the time. You do not need anything else—no altar, incense candles, gurus, gods, sacred texts, structures, or specific locations—to connect to yourself. The love is emanating from you to you. **Many religions have tried to convince you that you need to be part of the structure to experience love. From our perspective, that is as valid as asking you to pay for the air that you breathe.** It is a natural part of you being you. It is the "I am that I am." You are all a part of God and are able to experience the magnificence without needing anything. It is built in. It is, however, your grand mission to discover it and to live it. Your institutions and leaders have known this fact for millennia and have tried to channel this yearning and this innate ability to gain political power and control over you. There is no outside source that is required to connect you with you. It is as if you needed someone to teach you how to breathe air and then to have you pay for it. It is if salesmen claimed that only if you adhere to their AIR, and breathe it in their building, would you be able to live.

We love you so because we know that you came here to discover what is shielded from you. The truth is so transparent—like air—and there is so much misunderstanding about it. There is never a judgment, because you are loved and you are eternal. We are your brothers and sisters. Some call us the "tutors of light," and we hold your hands and hug you. And so be it.

Open the Bag

WHEN YOU ARE ALONE, what is it that you most crave? From our perspective, it is the feeling of belonging. *Why do I need others?*, you may ask. *You* are *others*, is our answer. *What do you mean? I am an individual. I know who I am. I do this and that. I was born to so and so and I look like this and that.* We find it funny that you define yourself by what you do, those you were born to, and what you look like. These items you see yourself as, are all your costumes of duality. You are none of these things. This is only your role. It is as if the actor in a play believes that he is his role. When we see you, we see your eternal essence. We see you as a cluster of stars brilliant in their glow. You are magnificent from our perspective. As you walk in your daily life there is a link that connects you at all times to all the other "clusters." Together, you shine brilliantly. It is an awesome sight. There is a link that all of you have. You share a portion of this cluster of "stars" with all other "clusters of stars." There are parts of you that wander from you to others and link all of you together. Parts of you contain all of humanity and life. It is the duality that separates you from other things and gives you the illusion that you are not a part of life. You do not have to be a famous person or to participate in any social activity to be part of the flow of life. You are part of this flow, and it is part of you.

As we see you, you are all connected. You cannot see the connection because of the veil of duality. It shields you from "seeing" the link. You can be hidden in a dark closet or under a blanket, and you are still connected to all of life, all the time. You are never alone. That is why we love you so much. It is as if you have chosen not to see, not to hear, not to smell, not to touch, and yet you are committed to finding the treasure. That is in our view a sacred mission, and an honored one. You and we celebrate your journey regardless if you have found the treasure or not.

Why do I feel depressed often?, some of you may ask. *Why do I feel so separated from other people? Why do I feel that no one cares for me? I feel abandoned.* We wish to tell you that it is a time of reunion of sorts. You have been separated from "you" for a long time, and now is the time to reunite with yourself.

The feeling of loneliness is from the connection to you. You have abandoned yourself. Many of you have followed your costumes and believed in your roles, only to find that the role did not carry substance. Some of you looked elsewhere for the eternal beautiful substance that makes you

who you are. Many of you have pursued the wrong treasure or a false one. This process was a test. Some of you have followed whatever looked the shiniest and did not look at the brightest jewel of all, the one hiding inside of you.

Do you wonder why we love you so much? Do you wonder why we tell you that there are trillions of us watching every move that you make? We hold your hand and just wait for you to call on us. You are on a sacred search second to none in the universe. This is how unique it is. You have the choice, and you are given the tools of yearning. You know that there is something you want, you feel the passion, you feel the desire, you feel the longing. And then you do not have the faintest idea what it is that you are looking for. You try to find it in other people, you look for it in things, you follow ideas, and you even attribute it to God. And yet all that time that you are trying to search and fulfill that yearning, the answer is carried inside of you in a bag. On that bag inside of you there is a little note with two words taped to it. *What is it?*, you may ask. *How do I open this bag? Will the note be written in my native language? Will I need a translation?* We want to assure you that you will be able to read the note, because the note simply says "open me." Those who have opened the bag have found that there are no more questions necessary as they found the answer to all their yearnings, longings, and desires. They found the love that they were always looking for. They found the love within themselves. When they walk the streets they change everyone's vibrations. Even if you do not notice anything special, you feel the stream of that link surging through you and connecting you to all that is. They are the holders of the magnetic fields of humanity. They are not beautiful in the way you describe beautiful, and they are not powerful the way you may define power, but they hold you and all of humanity linked in an invisible string because they discovered the "I am that I am." They know that we are all one—you and us and all of life. They also know that whatever manifests in the outer reality is just a manifestation of the inner growth that we need to reach. It is just the course of study we are currently on. They know that they are loved always and they are never alone. They know that all the misery in the world and all the pain is a manifestation of our individual role, and it is of our choosing. They walk with love, hand in hand. They walk connected to the love source inside of them, because they found the treasure. They are angels dressed up as regular people.

It is we who serve you. It is you who do the work. We are light beings, just like you. We are angels, just like you. We are very close to you, yet hidden. We can feel your breath. We often touch you lightly, just to let you know that we are close. You cannot see us, but at times you can smell us. Some of you can hear us as a melody or a sound; we are a subtle vibration. We are in harmony with all that is. Where we come from there is never a conflict. We do not battle the dark, because it does not exist; darkness is simply lack of light. Where we come from all the rooms are well lit. **When you walk feeling lonely, you are in darkness. When you feel not loved, you are in darkness. It is not an evil attribute. It is the attribute of an angel who lost touch with its divinity. Darkness is a cut between you and you. The more you separate from yourself, the darker shade you take.** However, the divinity inside of you always stays on. It is the human walking on earth in duality that has the power to choose whether he wishes to connect to that light within, or separate from it. Even the most evil person ever to walk the earth still carries the light of divinity inside. It is the other part that chooses to separate from that light and claim the darkness.

For the human to choose darkness, he needs to intentionally close his eyes, as light is your natural state. When you open your eyes, the light reflected from the object in front of you shows you who you are. We are the tutors of light; we love you. We wish you to open your eyes at this time. This is a time for great celebration. It is a time when the distance between you and you is shrinking. The curtain that hides you from yourself is becoming thinner by the day. We ask that you give yourself a hug and introduce yourself. When you feel the love, you will know that you have reunited with "you." And so be it.

The Mother-In-Law

I T IS HERE AGAIN.

What is here again?, you may ask. The celebration of death and re-birth is our answer. It is a symbolic world you live in. Your celebration, from our perspective, is an opportunity to shift energy, to make a change in your life, to take a break and look back. Holidays are a time of reflection. We wish you to live your life in a state of continual holiday. When you stop to reflect, or whenever you slow down, those things that seemed to be so urgent, important, and useful fade to the background, and your human relationships float to the foreground. It is relationships we wish to speak to you about.

We ask you to let go. *Let go of what?*, you may ask. Let go of the ideas you have about relationships. *Why?*, you may ask. *All my misery comes from a relentless insensitive boss, an abusive partner, a gossipy mother-in-law*, and so the list goes. What we ask of you is to let go of the idea that the problems you are facing come from those relationships you have. We look at you with so much love as we see you being burdened by all these seemingly arbitrary personalities who cause you pain. Some of you dream at night and wish that these people who hurt you would disappear. There are some of you who dream that if only they did not have this or that relative, parent, sibling, uncle, aunt, or co-worker who make their life so difficult or that if you could just "exchange" this person with that person, like you do with Christmas gifts, your life would be so much better. We hear you thinking to yourself: "Let me just change one and all will be perfect." We wish to tell you that it is perfect. It is always perfect.

When we hug you and hold your hand, we see the sacredness that each of these relationships holds. We want to promise you that not a single one of these people who plays a part in your life to the positive or negative is there by accident. Each relationship you have consists of a color, or hue; it also has a melody, a distinct smell, and a specific geometric shape.

Your relationships are your biggest assets. Your relationships are your fortune. As you negotiate your relationships, so your colors and shapes change. As you interact with these relationships, you create music. Each interaction creates a vibration. It is a vibration on various dimensions. It is beautiful to us. Many come from the far distance of the universe to learn from you about your human relationships. It is indeed your treasure.

Why treasure? For me it is just a drain, you say. *I could be so peaceful and yet I am nervous when I am in a relationship. It causes me anxiety and sleepless nights. When I am by myself I feel in peace.* You came here to grow and learn is our answer. That was your original intention. You came with contracts. Those contracts are signed by you and the other relationships around you. There is not a single relationship within all this web of life that was not there at the signing ceremony. It was and is a sacred ceremony. You hugged each other and promised to help each other learn and grow. You promised each other to hold sacred this commitment. Each of you signed these contracts with a golden pen, and the word "love" was followed by each of your spiritual names. This ceremony is indeed an awesome sight. No matter when and in what circumstances someone enters into your life and creates a change in you, they may have created a test for you or a challenge; they may not even know your name, but they caused you to become angry, sad, or frustrated, so be sure that they were at the ceremony.

We wish to tell with all love that your higher part, and the higher part of the one who may cause you grief, are together in a quantum state in a different dimension and you both metaphorically hold hands and hug while planning how to bring about change and learning in the two of you. There are those of you who "accidentally stumble" upon a person who causes a gigantic drama in your life and you are regretting the moment you ever stepped out of your house that day. As you are linear, you may feel that it does not make sense because you just happened to meet that person by chance and it happened only because the "baby sitter canceled on you," for example. From where we stand, holding your hands, we wish to tell you that it was no accident. The drama caused by a seemingly arbitrary stranger was planned by you and the stranger in a quantum state. We see the planning that goes into each of these interactions. It happens in a world or reality void of time. Time only exists in physical reality. The planning takes place outside the scope of time. One second is eternity, and 100 years is one second. As you walk the streets in your daily life, the planning takes place 24/7. The plans change and shift based on your choices, your lessons, and your reactions; it is a work in progress. It is a work of art made of colors, melodies, and shapes that are moving in perfect harmony. For you, the reality of all these relationships is shielded from you; the reasons are hidden. You have to face them without the why. It all may seem so arbitrary. At the same time the part of you that is not with you is sitting with many other energies that are part of your relationships. They all love each other. You and they are working out the details of each of the lessons. All of the lessons are tests of sort. Because you are the planner as well as the executioner, there is no test that is devised to fail you. You can pass all of the tests with honors. After all, you would not create a test for yourself that you had no chance to pass. The part of you that is "Godlike" is linked to the part of you that is an angel disguised as a human. You walk hand in hand creating challenges, opportunities to grow and learn. Your learning always is to find the signature in gold that is written in spiritual script and spells the word "love."

You create a masterpiece every time you say to yourself; *I found peace in this relationship. I no longer need to use anger because I understand the sacredness of it. I understand my role. I know why it was given to me and I thank myself for the opportunity to learn. I thank spirit for the ingenuity it disguised in the signature of Love from my relationships.* When you thank the one who hurts you for being your teacher of compassion, then you become the one who changes the actual magnetic fields of the earth you walk on. As you walk on grass, the grass knows who you are and it bows to greet you because it is honored by your presence. The trees that cover your road know who you are. When you become peaceful, you literally create a change on the planet noticed by every living creature.

You do not have to stay with a person who hurts you. Some of you hold on to the memories of those who hurt you, and you keep living the memory of pain staying in the place of victim-hood. It is through balance that you can let go of physical relationships if you so choose. When the learning is achieved, you no longer need the lesson. It is then that you move on without needing to repeat. You always have a choice. Whether you stay or leave a relationship, the steps stay the same: become peaceful, recognize the love signature, and express gratitude for the lesson. That is why your relationships are your treasure.

So how do I make peace with all these relationships? What do I need to do? Where do I begin? As we love you and walk with you hand in hand without judgment, we wish you to do the same with your relationships. Your first step is to become aware that it is through a contract of love that this challenge was created and to suspend your judgment.

Become peaceful with it and hold yourself with love, realizing that you have designed it for you. As we watch you interact, we see you interacting with other parts of you. All the conflicts created are inner conflicts manifested so they can be expressed and resolved. It is "you" learning about "you" that is bringing all these relationships into your life so you can explore in depth the meaning of being a human. Through your exploration, you develop your soul. Whenever you become peaceful with aspects of yourself, the test is passed, and those relationships will no longer offer a negative feeling. It is the transformation that takes place inside of you that creates the energy that changes this planet's magnetic fields. All your relationships are an outward manifestation of your inner state.

All the aspects of the "arbitrary people," who seemingly popped into your life, are aspects of you who came to introduce themselves so you will know more about yourself. This process is beautiful. The harmony in the music that you create when you become peaceful with a contentious relationship is magnificent. And you are so dearly loved for walking the walk. Your journey is honored, and you are never judged. We are honored when you ask us to help, and we are always with you. And so be it.

Change in the Final Act

NOWHERE IN THE UNIVERSE do you find the exact same experiment taking place as on your planet at this time. *How come?*, you may ask. *This universe is grand with many different worlds? Why are we different?* It is not you who is different. You come and go in different worlds. You know us, and we know you. So it is not you who is special. It is you and the planet at this time that is special. The shift that we are seeing is taking place on a grand scale. You have a very special part in it. *We still do not understand. Why special?* you ask. This experiment was on one path, and now it is on another. It shifted when everybody thought that it was about to end. In the grand finale of the last act, something magical happened. That something was "you." You have chosen to continue something that had the final act written all over it. You sailed into uncharted waters. There is no script, no rehearsal, because you changed the ending of the final act and chose to continue the play. Your choice surprised many, and it created a ripple that echoed in the entire universe. Is it special enough for you?

There are those who come from far distances just to look at you and observe what you are doing. You are exotic to many. There are many of us watching for each one of you. All of us who watch you do not interact with your day to day. We are not allowed, as it is a place of free choice honored and revered. There are some who may interact with you, but not us. It is a complex system. We are like you, as we are made out of light and energy. Our essence is love just like you. We are your helpers at this time. We volunteered to do so because we love you so much. There is no greater gift for us than to help you. We do not visit this planet in physical bodies. Our mission is to take your hand and to light your path, to nudge you a little and to love you a lot. We are your tutors if you ask for our help.

We feel you and we know who you are. We also know how you feel. Some of you are very brave. You have taken the more difficult option. That option is of mastery and ascension. It is not an easy path. You could have easily said goodbye in the last act, bowed, and returned home. You have chosen, however, to remain with love, to stay balanced, to keep the light on. You have set an example that vibrated the fabric of the universe and thus have set the stage for something even greater, and then even greater than that.

You do not know where you are going because you have designed it that way. You had a challenge to select the dark or the light. Your selection is recorded in the energy of earth. When the measurement of earth's energy was taken, the balance favored light. Such was not always the case. Free choice is honored above all. Darkness is neither good nor bad; it is just an aspect of the light.

The animals, the trees, the bushes, the rivers, and the sky all know your decision. Everything around you vibrates with newness. The storms, the earthquakes, the fires, the wind all know of this great shift. All these energies are aligning with you. As you change, so does the world around you. Many of you feel that you want to return home. You feel tired, confused. It's true that many of you chose to change the energy, but there are still many who remained with the final act. They rehearsed for it, and they planned for it for a long time. They know their last words and they wish to see it through, no matter what. Their choices are honored and never judged.

You see, all of you will come back to Earth. When you are not here, you are with us and you are so in love with Gaia and humanity that all you can talk about is coming back. You do your study, and you stand in line so you can return as quickly as you can. All of you knew the reality of living on this planet. After all, you have done it many times before. However, this time is different. Everyone wants to be here for the final act. This is where the main actors bow to the spectators. There are those who do not wish to improvise and to move into new, unknown energy. There are those who choose to reenact the final episode alone. Their wishes are honored. It is like a game and some feel that they will do better to start over. Many of you feel that it is the most important game you have ever played and you wish to live every moment of it.

We want to hold your hand so you can slow down. You think that if you move faster, you will get somewhere and can then relax. It as if the hamsters will arrive sooner by spinning on the carousel more quickly. We wish you to enjoy the ride. You have done many of these cycles before, but this one is for the record. You are doing something that no one predicted you would do. Your biology is changing, your DNA is changing, the earth's magnetic fields are changing, even the constellations are changing, and it is all because of you. So we wish you to slow down, keep yourself balanced. Find the joy and hold it in. From where we stand, there is a great commotion now on earth. There are new colors, new vibrations, and new melodies. Those who come from far away are here to hold your hands; the masters who walked the earth are here to hold your hands. You have so much support if you choose to accept it. We see turmoil, and we see peace. We see love, and we see anger. We ask you to slow down so you can integrate the energy coming into your system. Allow it to be absorbed and your biology to change. You think that you need to do everything by yourself, but from our perspective it is not the case. There is much help coming in. Your task is to become sensitive to the subtle messages that you are receiving. Use love in all your decisions and move slowly. It is time to walk as if you were a blind man with a stick. Walk slowly and feel your way around. What you see with your eyes may show you a picture that can steer you away from the truth. Feel your truth and slow down.

Your biology is used to one speed, so it takes time to readjust itself. Many of you feel that if you do not read about everything happening in the world you are missing something. We are here to love you and to reassure you that what you watch on TV and read in newspapers doesn't begin to tell the true story. We see how the colors and vibrations you are being fed carry the seeds of fear. Fear is your greatest challenge at this time. We ask you to go inside and not to look outside for the information. It is the balanced human who sends light. It is the fearful human who oozes darkness. We ask you to go on a diet and to become very choosy with those things you allow into your awareness.

Your reality is not made out of one linear dimension. You create your own reality based on your choices and interpretations. We love you, and we are here to hold your hand. And so be it.

You and Your Body
are Teammates

I S T H E R E A T I M E when you feel that you are tired?
You have a vehicle, your body, and it is a precious one.
You are responsible for your vehicle for your journey's
duration. Who do you think will take care of it if not
you?

As we look at you from above, and at times from below, we see those who are abusing their vehicles. You
fuel them with the wrong gasoline; you oil them with the
wrong lubricant. And you buff them with the wrong wax.
Why are you wondering, then, that you feel the way you
feel? The irony we are seeing is that when you purchase
a new vehicle, a real one, you read the instructions and
follow the maintenance program closely. You use the
correct oil and surely the correct gasoline, but when it
is your body you are dealing with, you think differently.
Then you are surprised when you fall ill. You are mad at
yourself for being tired, and you are puzzled that you are
required to go to the garage and have your parts replaced
and worked on from time to time.

Some of you like to think that you are separated from your body. Some of you like to think that your body is responsible to carry you throughout your journey, no matter what. The way we see it is that you have a relationship. The relationship is not only with the mechanics of tissue, blood, and bones put together. It is also with another intelligent consciousness. Your relationship is between one consciousness and another. You have a group that is "you" cooperating and working within a group that is your body. Your body is a group that operates under a skin in the physical dimension. The other "you" acts as a link between the physical dimension and the spiritual, astral, and other dimensions.

You and your body are teammates. You share the same goal and you come together to work as one. It is indeed a sacred union that you have with the group that you call your body. Would you treat your teammate with disrespect before an important game? Would you give your teammate the wrong sports shoes to wear before that big game? If you were the coach, would you feed the team the wrong kind of food so the team will be without energy when it faces its opponents? Your answer, most likely, would be, *I would never do that to my team. I want them to win, so why would I mistreat them before a game?* Many of you are sports fans. We take special delight watching you during a game of sports. Your emotions are high, and your enthusiasm is contagious. You love your sport heroes, and you pay good money to go to the games. You take the time to watch them on your TV. You support them with your prayers and get upset when the coach makes a mistake. At the same time that you watch the game you ingest the kind of food that drains your other teammate, your body, from vital energy and from life force.

It is ironic to us that you support those who are outside yourselves and abuse those who are your own. We know who you are, and we love you. Some of you have karmic accounts to settle and the sickness that you are experiencing is a part of that energy. Some of you have a learning that is intense, and you choose it to be manifested through physical ailments and limitations. There are those who need to learn to receive, so their soul chose to be in a body that is crippled so they can learn this aspect in this cycle. We wish to talk to those who came this time around with a healthy potential, yet are choosing sickness. It is a time like never before, where the consciousness that is your body is in constant communication with you. It knows your intentions, and it knows when you fuel it with the wrong kind of liquids. It responds to that. A car that is supposed to work on highly refined octane and is being fueled with low-octane, rate fuel will perform at less than its potential.

We know who you are, and we love you so very much. We see the fear in your eyes when something that you do not know grows inside of you, but then you continue to feed that growth with the wrong kind of substances. We want to tell you that your body responds to your instructions. It is your teammate, and it is sworn to follow your instructions. You are a teammate and a coach combined. When you tell your body that you have low expectations from it, it will respond. When you tell your body that you do not expect to live very long, it will respond. It can hear you. It walks with you every day, and it knows that you are the coach. It also knows what it needs. Your teammate knows what kind of fuel it needs. It is recorded in its manual. Each cell knows what it needs, and it can communicate it to the coach if the coach asks.

Your body is the way you choose to express yourself in the most magnificent creative event ever. You are the conductor, and your cells are the musicians. If you conduct well, the music will be divine. When you are healthy, you emanate energy that is vital, happy, and powerful. When you have strong life force, you can change things that you do not like. You can create the reality that you want. The colors and shapes that define your energy are governed by your life force. Your life force energy is the energy that propels you to move within the trajectory of your groove or change trajectory all together. Your groove is your karma. **When you begin the spiritual process we call ascension, you require energy. The process of ascension has to do with moving away from your karma or your groove and**

charting a new, magnificent path. We ask you to connect the dots between your spiritual journey and your physical life force, as it must be intact and powerful for you to move forward.

The vital energy that is at your disposal is the tool to vibrate higher and to resolve issues that you considered impossible. Everything that you do as you walk the walk on earth requires energy. Your energy center is your body. It is your engine. You can feed it all the wrong fuel and abuse it, yet it will remain loyal to you. It will still function and serve you, but why would you want it to work so hard and to move so slowly when it can have ease and fly?

It is your choice—the conductor, the coach, and the teammate to look after and guide your body to its highest performance. *How do we know what is good for our bodies?* you may ask. *We try to do the right thing, but still our body is getting more and more tired,* you say. **If you feel that something is wrong for you, then it is. Listen to your body, watch it, observe it, and love it like you love your favorite teammate. Your body will respond. It is not the food that makes the greatest difference; it is the intention. As you listen and pay attention, you tell your body that it matters. You renew your vows and let it know that you are committed to your partnership. Your body will respond.** The vibration that you send is more powerful than the enzyme in the food. It is the intention you vibrate that harmonizes with you. The fuel is a metaphor for intention. Speak to your body; honor it when it functions well. Attend to it when it is weak. Listen to it and allow it rest when it needs to recuperate. Honor your relationships, and you will be honored with longer life, vitality, and joy. You came here this time around for a special mission. We wish to hold your hand and light your path. It is indeed a special time and we wish you to celebrate it with us and we love you so. And so be it.

The Pilot Light

THE DECISION TO BE A PART of this play is entirely yours. You are never forced to participate against your will. There are those who say, *I do not feel that way. I did not choose to be here.* Some of you say *I want it to be over. It is not the ride I thought it would be. I had so many dreams as a child and I have no dreams anymore. I am just waiting for the nightmare to be over.* We wish you could see the beauty of your journey. We wish you could see the landscape that we see. There are those who say, *I see only trash on the streets. I encounter aggression daily. I meet people who try to hurt me. I feel like a loser.* We honor you, too, is our answer. **The love of spirit is such that even though you feel that there's only darkness around you, you are still loved. Even when you create darkness in your daily life, the light inside of you is always there waiting for you to choose it. Such is the love of spirit. It is always available to hug you at any moment.** You can distrust it, you can believe that there is nothing there; you may feel that there is only darkness and still the light remains unfazed, waiting for you to choose it when you feel ready.

It is not the intention of spirit to force you into happiness, balance, and joy. Such force would go against the contract you signed when you came here. You wanted to be challenged. Do you remember what you said before you descended into the birth canal? You said *I am ready and willing to face this challenge.* You were congratulated by the multitudes, and you smiled when you stepped into the vortex that brought you into this life. You knew how precious the gift of life was. You still do. You have just forgotten temporarily. Some of you go through each day feeling victimized and waiting for the end. Do you realize that as soon as you get to the end you will stand in line to get back into the game and start over? All the things that weigh heavy on you are not who you are. They are decorations that can be discarded at any moment. There are those of you who claim you are stuck. As we love you so, we whisper in your ear that the stuck-ness you feel is you holding onto this feeling of being stuck.

Many of you are so afraid to let go of the "bad" feelings because it feels so familiar. We know who you are. You have ground yourselves for so many lives—smelling the dirt, being abused, being hurt, betrayed, punished, prosecuted, executed—that you feel at home with being a victim. There are those who have come this time around with the firm commitment to change, to let go of the past, to discover the love within, and the divinity in your cells. You have been given opportunity after opportunity to choose that which fulfills your promise and yet you choose that which is familiar. As we love you, we see the light inside of you waiting to be ignited. Inside all of you there is a pilot light that holds your eternal flame. Your task is simple: turn the dial and let the flame soar; turn your light as high as you can. The flame is waiting and the dial is inside of you, so we ask you with all love, what is it that you are waiting for? *These are just words*, some of you say. *We do not see any flame, nor can we see the dial. All we see are vicious human beings.* Your eyes are seeing from the reflection of your insides. You choose to see darkness and you tell yourself that this is your reality, so why make an effort? We see reality that is grand and you see a reality that is dim. Why is it so? You see what you choose to see. You take in what feels comfortable for you. If you come from darkness, you will see only darkness. When you come from light, you will see light in everything. We ask you to start by observing the pilot light that is inside of you. There is no darkness that can put out your pilot light. It is your gift from spirit and it is yours for the duration. You always have the choice. It is waiting at any given moment.

I am too old to try something new, some of you say. How about eternity? Do you wish to start from where you left off? This is how it works. Victim-hood is a choice. You can choose mastery a day before you complete the game and go home, and it is not too late. We are your brothers and sisters, and we love you. All we wish to do is hug you and allow you to see the light inside you so you can experience the love of spirit. When you feel the love within, a second lasts forever. It is a feeling that can never happen too late. We know who you are. Many of you experienced it a moment before you stepped out of the play. Many of you have made a promise to yourselves to discover it earlier this time around. You are eternal. You are the "I am that I am." You came here to change what was and create new. You are an artist who stands in front of a white canvas moment by moment. Any moment is a new canvas from which a masterpiece can be created.

When we see a cloud in the sky, we know that the sun is shining above it. The sun shines regardless if you see it or not. We offer you a ticket to board the plane and soar above the clouds where the sun shines all the time. Moreover, when on the plane you can choose to fly in the direction of the sun and experience it all the time. The sun shines whether you believe in it or not. It is the same with the light within you. It is your sun. *How do I get the ticket?*, some of you ask. *I am poor. I have no money at the moment. Only the rich can get that ticket. We are sure it is unaffordable.* Our answer to you is, again, you choose to be the victim, and again we love you. We already covered it once. Will you choose it again and again, only to discover that the ticket to that airplane is not only free, but it also is part of your birthright? You came with it for life. It is written in your spiritual name. It is who you really are. You are the pilot, the plane, and the passenger. That is how magnificent you are. You can choose to soar at any given moment. It is a special time now and the light that you have is waiting for your intention. As we come into a new year, make your cells know that the time has come to move from victim-hood to master-hood and we love you so. And so be it.

The Old and the New

I F WE WERE TO CONGRATULATE YOU, it would be for the fact that you are here now. Nowhere and no time have been just like here and now on your planet. You are at a crossroad between old to new. What you experience in your daily life is the tug of war of light and dark pushing and pulling at each other, disguised as shades of grey. The shade of grey fluctuates within you and outside of you, moment by moment. There is tug of war inside of you that manifests outside of you. It is the old making space, sometimes reluctantly, for the new. The old does not want to leave, so it anchors itself and at times even pretends to be the new.

How am I doing?, you may ask. You are walking the walk, we say, and we congratulate you on every step. You knew it would not be easy. After all, you have been here before and you have walked the walk many times. Before you came this time around, you said that this time would be different. *How come?*, some of you may ask. Before now, you could not see, hear, or smell, and it was OK with you. Now slowly your old senses, the ones you lost a long time ago, are returning to you and if you choose to, you are able to see, and even know, what it is that you are seeing. At no time on your planet in your current biology were you as enabled as now. The hills and the desert, the trees and the animals are changing as you change. They can "see" also. They show you where to go and what path to take. As you move from old to new, you will see changes in the planetary life and in the animals' life on this planet. They will give you clues as to what is going on. It is time to reconnect with them as they represent Gaia.

As you are on the eve of completion of a year and a new beginning of a year, you are seeing all around you the swirling of energy. There is much turmoil all around, there is insecurity, there is fear, and there is pain. We know who you are. As you cross from a nine year to a one year, the old is giving in to the new. Nine is the energy of completion, and one is the energy of new beginning. It is the way things are being done that is changing. **What used to work in the past will no longer work as well. The swirling of energy will not leave anything where it was. This energy is the energy of ascension and it is powerful. It takes you upward on a journey that requires trust and fearlessness.** You have bought the ticket far, far in advance and you have waited for this moment your whole life.

You knew about this journey even thousands of years ago. *How come?*, you ask. *It is all new to me.* Our answer is that you knew of the potential and you signed on, each and every one of you. There are no signs, and there are no directions to where you are going now. It is determined by your intent. The path manifests as you walk. It is the most glorious of all to be walking in a territory so unfamiliar that it is a surprise even to spirit. We are with you all the time and we love you. It is our promise to you. When you came this time around, the old energy was powerful and the new energy was beginning to express itself on this planet. Most of you were alive when that process began. We are talking about changes that are so big and yet they just happened. They are happening now.

Can you explain to us the difference between the old and the new?, some of you may ask. It is the difference between a newborn baby and an adult. You were helpless laying on your backs, being moved around by others, being fed, being dressed, and you had no real ability to chart your own will and to do what you came here to do. The difference is that within a short period of time you became like an adult. With it comes the responsibility of an adult. The difference is your access to yourselves. The difference is in your level of awareness and your vibration. As you move, you no longer move like a baby throwing your hands toward a toy, sometimes hitting it and sometimes missing it. Now you are able to pick up the toy and play with it and use it to learn and grow. The energy coming to you is changing your biology in such a way that your senses work differently. The younger generation is now so much more equipped than the older ones to absorb the new rays. You will see new breeds of consciousness coming to the planet as newborn babies. They come with gifts that some of you have to work hard to attain. This is an exciting time. It is a pivotal time.

MESSAGE CONTINUED ON 1/1/08 NEW YORK

Where have you been hiding?, you have asked us. We are here and we ask you to open up so you can "feel" us. There is communication between us all the time. There are dots and commas to each sentence. We are the spaces between the words. We ask you to pay attention to the empty. The quiet is where the action is. Find the quiet corner and you will feel the strings that connect us. If your mind is in the future, you are not with us and if you are in the past, you are not with us. To be with the connection you must be in the here and now. The empty space is at the end of the exhale when you breathe out. It is when stillness allows the substance to come forth. We are subtle and so are you. Yet, since you must deal with being in a body, we wish to teach you how to maintain a connection despite the heaviness you carry.

Your body is a tool and you operate through it. It is when you quiet the body that the subtle vibrations can be felt. *Why are you telling me this?*, you may ask. Light and heavy are the feelings you must look for when you decipher between old and new energy. The old and the new are the same energy transformed. It is like water turning into ice or steam. New energy from old energy is simply a change in consistency. As the vibration of your planet changes, as your and earth's magnetic fields change, so do the rules of the game you are playing. Some actions that hold a certain vibration are no longer supported by this new vibration. Some actions are supported differently. It is not that the old is bad and the new is good. The old used to be the only game in town and now the new is replacing the old. In the past there was only a certain set of rules that everyone had to play under. Now there are two sets of rules. The old sets still work at times but less and less so. The new rules are taking over and those who read the new manual and feel the changes can manage their daily lives in more harmony. Children come to earth with the new set of rules already attached, so they do not need to work so hard to adjust. It is like lighting a path with your flashlight as you walk by a certain area. The path is dark; you light it, and when you move on it goes back to dark. The old was the darkness that was always there and the new is you lighting your path. You no longer need the flashlight. You are the light and as you walk by, your inner light transforms the old into the new. We wish to tell you how the old energy feels compared to the new. The old energy has to do with the energy of control. It is also the energy of fear. The old energy is wrapped in manipulation. Many of the old energy ways have to do with channeling you to do something that does not serve you, so you will not "see" who you are. In the old energy, you had to have everything translated so you could understand true from false. In the new energy, you do not need translations as you will observe that false sounds like false and truth will harmonize with you. You will be able to see it. The new is light and there is no control of one over the other. It is the energy of cooperation, it is the energy that allows the love vibration to take over and show the path in all instances and actions. It is the energy of truth. Not a truth that holds one against the other, but truth that allows each individual to express their truth and flourish. Can you imagine such a world? The new is feminine and the old is masculine. The new is nurturing and the old is discipline-based. We wish to tell you that there will be a time when the difference between the ways of the old energy and the new energy will be so apparent that those angels who hold the vibration of the old energy will have a difficult time mixing with those angels who hold the vibration of the new energy and there will be a split.

That is not the case at the moment. You are at the crossroad of a change so vast that trillions of us observe you and are excited about the prospects of earth. The old and the new are still intermingled and your actions have both energies. It is your task to be in the here and now in order to maintain inner quietness so you can choose moment by moment the light versus the heavy, the free versus the controlled, and true versus false. You must work on the balance of your masculine and feminine sides so you can be comfortable in the new energy. The new is a feminine energy guided by intuition, where the old energy is masculine and guided by reason.

You have waited for this moment for millennia. It is so unique that we ask you to slow down so you can feel it. We know who you are and some of you are being impatient. It is time to slow down and feel your way around. Look for the dots and the commas. We are holding your hands and we wish you a glorious journey and so be it.

Bread Crumbs
on the Forest Floor

REGARDLESS OF WHERE YOU ARE and what you do, you are loved. There are those who believe that they are loved only if they bow down and read sacred script. There are still those who feel that if they do not perform a certain ritual, spirit will abandon them. There are those who feel guilty if they miss going to church on Sunday because they believe that God will get upset and not grant them their wishes. You have so many misunderstandings about God, and we wish to touch upon a few.

To begin with, you assign a personality and an identity to God: God gets upset, God avenges, God is not happy with this but is happy with that. It is humorous to us that you take something so grand and assign to it a limited scope of being.

Throughout history you have looked for God. You yearn for God because you feel that there must be something else out there. You know that it cannot be that what you see is all there is, and you are right. As you walk in your daily lives, many of you ask yourselves, *does God love me? Have I been good? Am I doing what it is that I am expected to do?* There are even those who feel that they betrayed God and that they will be punished as if God is some kind of a policing angel who tickets you if you do not do what you are supposed to do.

How do you know what God tells you? Your religious institutions will tell you that you have received books and sacred texts. They believe that these books have been written by God and therefore must be followed to the letter. No matter that some books were written hundreds or thousands of years ago; some of you still feel that they hold the same energy as they did when they were given by God.

Some of you have looked upon God as a friend and some as the almighty ruler who does what he wants and can bring joy or misery to his followers. There are still those who feel that God belongs to them and that the God of other belief systems is false. We are your brothers and sisters. We are with God all the time. When you are not walking on earth, you are with God all the time as well. You know who God is when you are not submerged in duality. It is you who take the hand of God when you come back home, and it is you who searches for that hand when you are separated walking on earth as an angel in plain clothes.

You think we do not see your wings? You come with that feeling of longing to God because you know it so well. It is part of you when you are on our side of things.

A metaphor that we can give you about your idea of God is as if you are walking inside a circular structure. It is a perfect circle, and yet you are looking for the beginning and you try to define the end. You are built that way. **God is outside your sensory ability. God's form exists beyond your perception and so you take that perfect circle and you chop it up so it will fit your reality. You build concepts, names, and ideas; on top of those you build ideologies, structures, hierarchies; at the top of everything you crown God as the ruler.** It is beautiful to us to look upon you and see how the test that you have designed, hiding God from yourself, is being played out. As the designer of the test, you have left yourself clues, and like Hansel and Gretel you have left bread crumbs on the forest floor, but the birds ate those crumbs and now you need a different vision to retrace your paths and find the way back to God.

We hug you and we wish to tell you about one of the most important attributes of God. God is the essence of love. It is the kind of love that never judges, never punishes,

and never asks anything from you. It is love and it is there always inside of you waiting to be discovered. The essence of God is in every cell of your body. It is part of you and it is a part of other billions and trillions like you. It encompasses all that is, and still it is felt in your heart when you decide to connect to it.

When you come to this planet, the first thing that you do when you emerge from your mother is to cry because you realize that you no longer feel as part of God.

The last thing you say before you go into the vortex that carries you to your earth destination is "this time I will find you." It is the attribute of your humanness that you often assign to God, so you can make sense of things.

We truly love you and we wish to tell you that one of the most important attributes of God is love. It is in the love that you feel when you are in love with someone. God is in the love a mother feels for her child. God is the essence of love, and that feeling vibration penetrates the veil of duality and it remains pure. It is the energy that remains constant between your reality of duality and our reality walking hand in hand with God. It is the vibration that bridges our dimension and yours. Why do we tell you that we love you? Because it is how we reach out to you and how you reach out to us. Love is a two-way communication between spirit and you. When you are in love with you, you are with God. Love is the feeling that transcends your linearity, and it is your link to the other side. When you connect with God, you are part of all things and all dimensions. The love feeling is not the type of love that is possessive, jealous, and limited to a space or a person. It is the energy that makes all that is, and it is the link to your own divinity. What surges through you and any other human walking on this planet is the love of God.

What about the "bad" people?, some of you ask. "They too", is our answer. When you are not here, you are part of that energy you call God. You are merged in that love feeling. Does it make sense to you that at the same time that you are merged with pure love essence you can be punished by that essence? This energy you call God is so grand and you are part of it when you leave earth. When you are in body, this essence resides in your body waiting to be discovered. Its energy encompasses the universe's essence of love. Earth is not the only planet, and you are not the only consciousness walking as humans.

There are millions of planets that carry the seed of God. All of them have the same substance surging through them. They are also your brothers and sisters, and you know all of them by name. Does it tell you a little about the energy you call God? It is so grand that the only way to understand it is through feeling. Your logical mind is limited, and it cannot conceive of God, but your heart and feeling centers are biased to know God. It is in the tears that the energy of God expresses itself. When you open the door hidden in you, this love fills you, then you touch God.

All the good and bad that some may attribute to God is your choice; the choice of the God portion of you, which directs your lessons this time around. The evil and darkness you encounter in your life is just a manifestation of your free choice. This is part of the test you have designed; "with free choice, what will you choose light or dark?" Darkness is available as well as luminosity, and the difference is that God does not exist in darkness, but only in light, and that the energy of love is the energy of light.

You are a divine being. You participate in the grandest of plays, and there are many in the universe who see your true colors. They sit in the audience and are in awe of your path. They are in love with you and some just come to learn from you as you walk in your daily life.

As you walk your path you must adhere to universal laws. One such law is the law of karma. The law of balance exists throughout the universe. Even God adheres to these laws. They are part of creation, and all actions move in accordance with these laws. Karma is the manifestation of the law of balance in your reality. As you walk and act in your cycles, you do things and make decisions. Those actions and choices carry an energy that must be balanced. This balance is the way you learn. When you walk in your karma, not one of you is separated from God. You may perceive a situation as "good" or "bad" or as positive or negative, but from where we stand it is all a fluctuation of energy through which you are learning and growing.

There are biases in the path of karma, and you may have guessed it, the bias is love and therefore God. The God within you voids karma. The balanced human no longer needs to learn through re-balancing past actions. The masters who walked the dirt of this planet moved away from their karmic path by being balanced. It is the key to your evolution. When you are balanced, the light that you emit is profound. The planet at this time requires light to move into the next dimension. There is no need to try to find God by going to a special place. There is only one place you need to go to and that place is inside of you. When you find the "I am that I am," and you feel the love that surges in your veins, you know that you are home. It is the most profound of feelings and the harmony that you create will resound in the entire universe, and that is why we love you. You carry inside of you the essence of love and so do we. And so be it.

The Big Boss

I S THERE ANYTHING THAT YOU FEEL that you need and do not have? *Of course*, most of you will answer. *I must have these things so I will feel better about myself.* Why is it that you need these things, we ask? *I need things so I can do things in the world? I need a phone, I need a house, I need a car, I need a family, I need.*

If you did not have any of these things, what would happen? Some of you will say, *I would feel like a loser. I would feel powerless. I would be nothing.* We wish to remind you that there was a time when you did not have any of these things and you were so powerful. *How could I be powerful without things?*, you may ask. Your power was inside of you and you knew how to use it. The more you forgot about your power, the more things you needed to help you feel powerful. He who needs nothing is the most powerful. When we see you doing the things you do, we do not see your gadgets. They are invisible to us because they do not emit the kind of frequency we are sensitive to. It is humorous to us that you feel that if you have an expensive car it makes you powerful. From where we stand, we do not even see the car. We can see your light and we can tell you that it has nothing to do with your gadgets.

What do you mean?, you will ask. *I have a boss who makes so much money and he can fire people and hire people and everyone respects him because he has a position and his word is powerful.* We wish to take you on a trip outside your linearity. We wish to observe the most important person in this business and the one who is in your opinion the meekest. We wish to take you on a metaphoric ride in our spaceship. We will hover above and observe the "big Boss" and the "meek" from behind the veil. We will try to describe to you what we see. You and we will see the colors green, purple, and light blue in an arch that resembles a rainbow. It is very special. Around the colors will be sparkles that seem to shine very bright and beside it a small cluster, dim and hazy. Imagine that these colors shift to pink and red and the sparkles spin in splendor while the other cluster remains hazy. This interaction is the powerful manager speaking to the meekest of this big business. We see the "powerful one" as a trail of a dim cluster of light and the meekest, who does not speak very good English and just arrived from a different country in search of a better life, as a bright galaxy of stars with beautiful colors that continuously change. The "meek" appears to us like your rock concerts at their best. The meekest emit the most light and colors.

When we love you, it is not because of your diamonds or cars or pretty faces. We do not even register that. We see you as pure energy. We see you the way you are, an angel, a piece of God. When we hug you we do not feel your fur coat or your designer outfit. We hug your heart; we embrace your soul. It is the physical costume that we do not register. That is our blind spot. We just see what you do with what you have. We see the reflection of your energetic movements. We see how each feeling, thought, and reaction manifests energetically and displays as a sound, light, and vibration. Some of you may say, *I do not understand. I am tired and powerless. I am old and unattractive and I do not have any money and surely no influence.* We hug you even tighter and love you even more, because we do not even see those things. We love you just for being there and walking the walk. We are light beings like you, and we are eternal like you. We see your actions as they are translated to frequency. For us, your actions and thoughts look similar. There is a slight fluctuation of frequency, but both have powerful vibrations. We do not know your earthly name or street address because we know your real name and your real home address.

You have been given a playground and within it there are rules that you must adhere to, a certain lesson that you came to learn, and it refers to all of you. We do not register your roles as you perceive them to be in your dimension; however, we see the reflection of the light that you create by making a thought or taking an action, which creates a certain vibration that changes your composition of light, color, sound, and vibration. The power that we see is always and only the power you exercise within. The power is held by those of you who are connected to the part you call the higher self, those who know their group and are in charge of the trillion of cells that carry the stamp of God in them. They are the powerful ones. We do not know if they drive a new Lexus or wear a big diamond ring. The power lies with recognizing all your parts and operating from a place that includes your inter-dimensionality. From where we see you, you shine like a huge sun. Your power comes when "you" unite with "you." The more you are with you, the more you are living the "I am that I am," and the more power you carry with you.

If you know who you are and at the same time you own a big business, that is well with us, and if you clean the streets that is well with us. You see, each role that you choose plays out a certain lesson that will allow you to move higher and expand your experience on earth. Your goal is to experience as much as you can and play as many parts, so you will be proficient with energy and creation. Your goal is not about money, fame, or power. These are simply some of the many tools you have in your sandbox. There are those of you who say, *that cannot be. We do not believe you. It is always the powerful ones who make things happen, and the meek that follow.*

Really?, we say. Do you know any powerful ones who stayed in power forever? Do you know any culture that dominated another forever? Who is remembered and influential over thousands of years? Are they the conquerors or the spiritual masters? When you look at your history, how many of the ones you call the villains won in the end? It is a game of dark and light, where free choice is the rule of the game. Within the game there are other rules that must be observed to make the game more interesting and to allow you to learn while playing it.

Do you know why this game is interesting? It is because you designed it for yourselves. The "things" some of you consider as important in your culture, such as money, influence, and sex, are all pure energies. You created these aspects so your test would be more "rich and versatile." Sex is energy that has light and dark polarity. When sexual energy is used correctly, it can introduce you to your highest realms and propel you to other dimensions and higher vibrations. When sexual energy is abused, it can lead you to the darkest corners of your humanness. Money is energy; again it is pure energy that doesn't have a good or a bad side.

Metaphorically, this energy is like a car full of gas and ready to be driven. It is not moving by itself. It is just there. When you the driver turn on the engine, decide on a destination, and release the brakes, that energy is being "flavored" with dark or light. There is no innate goodness or badness in any of your cultural or natural physical world. All is neutral waiting for the angel in plain cloth walking on earth to give the flavor, adding some darkness or some light. What we see from our theater seats is the light or darkness that you create when you think and act. It is not important to us which energy you use as much as the flavoring that you add to that energy.

It is, however, apparent that when you are passionate about something, you seem to be more linked with you and the sparks that you create are more beautiful. They sing differently. If you choose, however, to not use this energy or that energy because you feel that it carries a negative side, it is, from our perspective, like a person who chooses to drive a car with only three wheels because he believes that the fourth wheel carries a negative attribute. The car will not get anywhere with ease. There are those of you who choose not to deal with certain energies, and we can assure you that if you avoid them this time around, you will choose a lesson interacting with this energy that will face you squarely next time around. Your lesson is not about avoiding, but about transforming and learning how to use energies. When you avoid energy, you are missing the point altogether. There are those who choose to be poor because they believe money corrupts. From our perspective, they are not utilizing one of the most important tools they have been given to learn and grow.

There are those who choose not to use sexual energy. From our perspective, it is like using a car but taking out the engine. Sexual energy is the most powerful energy source you possess. The destination is your own choice. Those who choose to remove that energy from their lessons will have to walk rather then use the fast car they have been given. Many of you do not trust yourselves because you have been in other cycles and you have met this energy, and it hurt you. We want to tell you that it wasn't the energy that hurt you; it was you choosing to learn aspects of you, so you will know both sides of "you," the dark and the light. You can always choose. We see you in fear, we see you in doubt, we see you in lesson, and we wish to hold your hand and let you know that you are never alone. We wish to tell you to trust yourself, because you have the ultimate power over everything that takes place in your life. All lessons are your choice. As we hug you, we wish to let you know that skipping a lesson will not allow transformation; it will only delay growth. You must experiment with all aspects of energy, using your tools. This is how you learn about all aspects of you. This is the real marriage with spirit. And as we say goodbye, we wish to tell you that you are loved dearly and honored just for walking the walk and so be it.

Like a Marionette

I T WILL BE WHAT IT WILL BE. Some of you believe that your life is preordained and you have no say. Some of you believe that you have a fate that is destined and you just need to wait till the ride is over. **You think that you are being moved like a marionette. Some of you believe that others control your actions regardless of your wishes. When we tell you that you are powerful, it is because you are the creator. The need and ability to create is an innate part of who you are and it is your birthright. When you are without a body on this dimension, all you do is create.**

How can I create without a body?, you may ask. Our answer is that you create without your body anyway. It is the energy of the thought that propels matter and not the other way around. The same process holds true on our side of the veil. You create with thoughts. The way you use your energy is, however, much more refined. With a body you need to learn to merge the thought with the body so the body will communicate that thought harmoniously. It is always a challenge to meld the soul's energy with the body's crude physical tools. The older the soul, the easier this process becomes. Newer souls adjust with more difficulty as they orchestrate their body to the music of the lower vibrational frequencies around them.

You are not alone in learning the process of melding. You have a team attached to you. This team works on the macro-level and it helps connect and synthesize the brain's synapses to create connections. This job is a fine and delicate one, yet, for newer souls, crucial. Some new souls are first-timers on earth who have been operating on other systems for eons. They come to be with you because this is where, at this moment in the universe, the action is. They are like you, beings of light and a part of God. They have been working in other worlds, not necessarily on the same task. As they come in, their senses are not naturally wired as are those of some older souls. They require help in translating some of the signals that for some of you are natural. These newer souls are your brothers and sisters, but when you meet them on the street, you sometimes view them as "weird" or "strange." Some of them are very sensitive and have difficulty adjusting to the brutality they witness. They do not understand how angels can act the way we do. Some come from universes void of duality and of free choice.

Your planet is unique because you can choose dark over light. The work of creation happens on many dimensions. You are operating on many dimensions as well, but are aware of only one. Our mission at this time is to awaken you to the entire spectrum of dimensions you occupy and operate on. When we tell you that you are grand, we are not exaggerating.

If you think you are tired just from being on earth at this time, doing what you are doing, we understand you because we see the work that you do when you are asleep. Do you think that God is ever asleep? When you rest in one dimension, often you operate in another. *How can I be in one place and operate from another at the same time?*, you may ask. You do exist in many different realties and dimensions, but you are aware of only one. The higher part of you is aware of all your parts and is responsible for coordinating all parts. The part of you occupying the body is the one that makes decisions for the group. Even though you are walking in duality, not remembering your true identity and mission, you are still as powerful.

This is the test. Your awareness has been shielded and hidden from you, but your power to create remains unshielded. Why do you think there is a powerful dark side to your world? It is because you created it. You are able to manifest whatever it is you wish for. You may ask, *why, then, were we given the power to create darkness?* Our answer is that you are loved so much for making this test "real." You are a powerful creator shielded from your true identity. You wanted to test yourselves to see, if left alone to create whatever it is you wished, whether you would create more light or more darkness. It is a simple, yet profound, experiment.

You are now at the end of the test, and it appears that you were about to fail, but then you changed course and instead you are about to graduate with honors. No one really expected it, and there was no judgment either way. It was all about the test. But as you changed your course, you changed everything around you. Now you are standing tired. Some of you, especially the "young ones" who do not know your rules too well, stand bewildered. You are in the midst of a battlefield, and there are many noises and explosions all around you. Some of you are afraid; others are worried. We wish to tell you that you are in a place so glorious that we have to shelter our eyes because of the new luminosity that earth is producing. It is a magnificent sight. To some, nothing makes sense. It seems like chaos. We want to remind you that we know you very well and you know us. We know what you are going through. We wish to tell you that all you need to do is move forward, one thought at a time.

We ask you to be in the now, because it is all you have. When you are in the now, you are the "I am that I am." When you are living in the past or future, you are immersed in duality. You are tainted by fear, anxiety, and hopelessness. It is the now that links you at every moment to your inter-dimensional self. It is all about you maintaining the communication with you. When you are creating in the now, you have nothing to worry about, because you are being guided.

It is when you say to us, please show me the way to go, that you allow us to come and assist you in your journey. All of us are just waiting for your signal. What you call spiritual teachings are more about listening than about doing.

You contain all you need, and you create what you need when you are in the now. When you are walking hand in hand with your breath, feeling your heartbeat, you are powerful. The joy comes from being you with you. There is no greater joy, because wherever you are and whatever you do, when you are linked to yourself, you are in bliss. When you are in bliss, you are the creator of your reality. On our side, when you create a flower petal, you see the results immediately. When you work in your "workshop" as angels creating life forms, creating stars, planets, and suns, time is not an issue. You are immersed in the now all the time. It is when you enter the dimension of earth that the clock starts ticking. The process of creating is similar. As you create, time comes in and delays results. At times, you do not even see the results of your creation in the same body. Some of you created magnificent things and had to experience them in later cycles, not even knowing their contribution to the creation. Do you wonder why, then, we are in awe of you? Do you wonder why we love you so and just wait for the opportunity to help you when you give us your hand? All you need to do is open your hand and say to us, "I am in the now, and I am ready to be shown what it is I need to see, what it is I need to do, and what it is I need to know."

We hug you all the time, but when you give us your hand, it is as if you hugged us back and then we celebrate with you. It is the marriage that we all yearn for. It is the meld of you acknowledging the other part of you. We love to co-create with you. It is your intention that sets us in motion and your state of being that allows us to fly with you. When you fly, you can see your journey from the perspective of your expanded self, and it is a grand one. And so be it.

The Crystal Ball

NO ONE CAN TELL THE FUTURE. Even the one you call God cannot tell you the future. It is you, the human walking the earth in duality, who always wants to know what the future holds. Why do you wish to know the future? The future cannot be told because if it could, the test you designed for yourselves would not be a test. It would be a sold game. You see all the potentials before you come here. You plan every possible scenario and you create situations in which you will have to face karma, challenges, and problems. It is all in your blueprint.

As you come to earth, you continue to plan. Do you think that the planning is finished once you arrive? The planning never stops, because you continue to change. The change that is occurring is all inside of you. As you change, and with every action and with every thought, so do your blueprints and plans.

You are eternal. You operate like us in a reality void of time. Time is a construct designed especially for you. It is part of the reality, of the lesson, you are in. It guarantees a constant movement and change. If you could operate in a reality void of time, there would be less of an incentive for you to grow, more so if you could see your past, present, and future. These aspects of reality must be hidden from you so you can exercise free choice. You are operating in a complicated web of possibilities, all floating in a vibrational field waiting to be activated. It is not the human who designed the test for its own evolution; the inter-dimensional group designed the test. It is you with your higher self, your guides, those who interacted with you in past lives, and even your cells that all are involved in the planning.

What you may call "the real" reasons for certain challenges in your life are hidden from you. It is always through the "link of love" that you are connected to your challenge. Those "tests" that you fear and wish to know in advance so you can prepare are the tools spirit uses to nudge you on your path toward spiritual growth. Some events are designed by appointments before you come. They are possibilities that you scheduled for yourself to remind yourself what is it that you came here to do. As painful as these events may seem, from our perspective they appear to be like a beautiful appointment between long lost friends. Some accidents, illnesses, traumatic events, and loss of loved ones are designed by you and co-created with others to bring you closer to your original self. You are dearly loved, and there is no force in the universe that wishes you harm. There are no negative powers that have a mission to put obstacles in your life and make your life more difficult. There are no angels of the dark. Angels consist of light, like us and you. The path you are on is a glorious one, but not an easy one. You come to a place with energy much denser than you are used to. You have to learn to operate a machine that uses crude ways to perceive the world. This machine is your body. You come with certain biases, like survival and fear. You operate within an almost hostile environment, and your mission is to find the subtle, the unseen. You are on a journey to discover things that you are not built biologically to discover. They need to be discovered within. Your bias tells you that your survival depends on your adaptability and ability to manipulate your environment, yet your real journey is about discovering the power within. It is an oxymoron. You must realize that learning the new skills and moving forward requires you first to unlearn what you have learned for millennium. It is not an easy task. **If you could peek into the crystal ball and know your future, it would mean that the future holds the answers and therefore the answers are not held by you.**

You are the master of your path, always. When you choose to let go of fear and to trust, you are changing one potential to another. When you choose not to use anger but to use love, you are changing one potential to another.

When you send blessings in your heart to the one who defamed you or hurt you, you are changing your potentials. How, then, can anyone tell where you're going? You are paving your path one reaction at a time, one step at a time. **As you move, the colors around you change, the geometric forms that you create change, the melody that you create changes, and everything around you responds to the changes in you. As you act, you create a domino effect. You find that love and peace changes the future for you and for the planet.**

Do you still feel that you are not powerful? You wish to know the future so you can be prepared. We wish to tell you the future. It is glorious. Always was and always will be. You are magnificent and you always will be. You always existed and will continue to forever. So what is it that you can possibly worry about? From our perspective, those who unlearn what humanity has taught them are the ones who are moving more quickly into the new energy.

The greatest learning is in the un-learning. There are those of you who believe you must fight to survive. Fighting for survival is no longer necessary. The new energy asks you to set intention to experience health, abundance and joy, and listen to your inner voice and trust it to lead you down the correct path.

How would some of you respond? You may say, *oh, this must be some kind of a conspiracy to take what we have and leave us behind.*

As we hug you, we wish to hold your hand and take you to a special place. You have called that place paradise. The garden of paradise holds all fruits in abundance. That garden is inside of you waiting to be activated. Trust in abundance creates abundance. The awareness of scarcity creates scarcity. It is your choice. We are with you everyday in the trenches, and we know who you are. We know what you have been through. We know the lives you had in which there was lack of food. We know of the lives you had as nomads in the desert in which water was scarce. We also know why you chose to experience these lives and the lessons you have learned. Those lessons, however, are hidden from you. **Even at that time in the desert, you had the power to create abundance. You are powerful in every environment. Your power to create is not dependent on the landscape; it comes from within. As you trust, you manifest trust. When you fear, you manifest fear. As you focus on survival, you will create the circumstances in which survival will be needed.** We wish you to experience abundance, because it is your natural state of being. Earth can supply you with all you need. The potential exists for a balanced planet in which every human has all he or she needs to experience abundance.

You may say, *how could that be? Look at the starvation in Africa. We have poverty here and there.* We love you and we wish to tell you that all conditions on earth can be transformed if you transform within. Your world is a reflection of your inner condition manifested in your outer reality. It is not the planet that is experiencing poverty, hopelessness, starvation, war, and famine, but the human who creates in a world of free choice that which he wishes. There are those of you who believe that with money and resources, poverty and famine will end. We wish to tell you that the only resources that can bring about peace on earth and everlasting abundance to all are the changes within individuals, one at a time. Those systems based on greed, exploitation, abuse, and lack of integrity will no longer be supported by the magnetics of your evolving planet. Those systems will begin to collapse and will be replaced by those that are carrying awareness of the new energy, the energy of cooperation, of trust, of integrity. We are here waiting for you to give us your hand. We celebrate each of you who let us in. We love you no matter what, but when you let us in it is a grand event. You may not believe that things can change in your life. You may feel that you are too old, or you have no capital to begin something. We wish to tell you that this journey is all about miracles. It is about transformation that is hidden from you because it is not linear. We ask you to allow these miracles into your life by trusting spirit.

Some of you may feel that you carry "bad karma" that prevents you from experiencing abundance. Karma, however, sets you off on a path of learning. The experience of poverty is no lighter or heavier than the experience of wealth. You must discover the power within and find peace, joy, and balance. Within that power, you will create abundance. There are those whom you call rich in your culture who drive expensive cars and wear expensive clothes. Many assume that these humans naturally experience abundance. From our theater viewpoint, this is not so. It is not the quantity of something by which we measure your abundance, but by the quality of your emotions in response to what you have. Are you fearful? Are you worried? Are you anxious? Can you laugh? Can you experience joy? When you walk in abundance, all the elements around you support your path. It is a knowing that is supported because it is balanced. Abundance is not about taking from someone else or competing, so one will have none and you will have all. Abundance is a state of equilibrium in which your needs are showered upon you with love and you are in balance with the planet and within yourself. And so be it.

Opening the Lockbox

THERE IS NO ONE quite like you. Each of you comes at this time for a specific mission. *What mission would that be?*, you might ask. *And how do we know our mission?* The key is waiting for you, and the lockbox is inside of you. Your mission is to find the key and open your lockbox. *What does the key looks like?*, you may ask. The key is your intent, and the lockbox spells LOVE all over it. *Will we be able to understand what is kept in the lockbox once we open it?*, you may ask. It is not in writing, but it is a fragrance that translates into a feeling hidden in the lockbox. Once you open it and inhale, the fragrance absorbs in your body and you change. *How do we change?*, you may ask. You evolve, your DNA changes, your vibration increases, and your pineal gland is being activated. Your biology comes alive and begins to communicate with your other parts. It is as if you were walking in the dark feeling your way by bumping into walls and by trial and error and all of a sudden someone turned on the light and you could see. Opening the lockbox enhances your abilities to move forward. You no longer walk in the dark not knowing the results of your actions and thoughts. You are connected to your biology and you know what your body needs to create health.

When you open the lockbox we can see you from a far-away distance, because of the radiance you emit. When we tell you that the planet emits so much light, we refer to those of you who opened your lockbox inside, smelled the fragrances, and became enhanced. The journey begins with intent. *Once we open the box, then what?* Your mission becomes clear. You can see because you turned on your light. The light emanates from within, so you no longer need a flashlight. **As you walk the planet in your biology, even in the darkest places your inner light is showing you the path. You cannot get lost anymore unless you choose to. The results of your walk become apparent as you walk. It is not about the future. Your path is about walking moment by moment in a certain vibration.** It is a high vibration that transmits a frequency that propels the earth to transform its current vibratory rate. As you walk and do the things that you do in your everyday lives, you fulfill your mission. You do not need to lecture or work in a specific institution. You are not asked to write a book or evangelize your wisdom. All you need to do is be. Walk as an enhanced human being on the streets, doing your life. As you walk the streets, you change everything as your vibration radiates through your magnetic fields. There will be those who will sense it and those who do not; nevertheless, they all change as a result of your "walking." It is as if there were an electrical outage and all of a sudden someone lights a torch and all those who were in the dark can see. They can still close their eyes if they wish to, but they have the option and they can now select to "see." When you open the lockbox, you are enabled and you allow others to be the same.

There are many of you who fear enablement because you do not want to know. You feel that knowing is too heavy. We say to you with all love that there is no judgment on you whether you choose to see or not. You are loved just the same. We know who you are. There are those of you who opened your lockbox in previous cycles and were burnt at the stake or tortured for carrying your light. You carry within you a cellular fear that activates your survival mode whenever you reach to that box. It is part of your journey and to have this fear is almost a prerequisite. You have experienced the different aspects of being a human. It is time to make peace with your cells. When you open the lockbox, the once-paralyzing fears are replaced by a fulfilling sense of balance and trust.

You have chosen to be here at this time for this very reason. It is your mission and you made a promise to yourselves not to allow fear to stir you away from fulfilling it. Now is the time. There is no other time in which every light ignited has such power. There are those who say, *I will wait this one out. I will see where the wind blows.*

I do not want to make any waves. We wish to tell you that it is no longer an option. You have to be with the old or with the new. If you do not choose the new, you are with the old. There is no middle way in which you can wait and see. The energy around your planet is changing rapidly. The magnetic fields and the vibrations are changing. Your biology is changing, and your consciousness is changing. If you sit idle, you will be forced to face a situation in which you will have to choose. It is energetic and not personal. It will be your higher part nudging you to move forward or you will stay behind.

There are many who feel that they do not want or are unable to change, and they want to find a way to get off the planet so they can come back more equipped as children. There is no judgment, but why would you want to miss the fireworks celebration? This is the most exciting of times on your planet. You have waited for millennium to be a part of what's taking place. It is the shift of all shifts and you want to be a baby while all of this is taking place? You are the one who made it happen. It is your mission to see it through and allow the shift to work through your consciousness down to Gaia. You are the vessel that allows those frequencies from the cosmos to go into the planet and change the magnetic fields.

Some of you are fearful. *It looks bad,* you say. We want you to come with us for a moment. Disconnect from all that is around you and come with us on the spiral of ascension and open your eyes. You will see something that will take your breath away. You will see a beautiful earth, balanced and loving. You will see tribes that fought each other for what seems like forever, sitting together and cooperating. You will see more abundance and fewer diseases. You will see joy coming from the face of the children, who intuitively know that the world is getting better with every passing moment. Does it look so scary to you? Do you want to miss it? We ask you to give yourself a hug everyday and congratulate yourself for being you. You are here and you are on the path that is honored and revered. It is up to you to find the lockbox inside of you and open it. It will allow you to experience more love and more joy than you have thought was possible. It will bring balance into your life, and it will diminish fear. As you open the box, you give your hand to the higher you and you no longer need to fear that you will lose your way. We wish to tell you that you are loved and through the love we transmit to you the fragrances that are stored in your lockbox. This scent is one you do not have on your planet. It is so unique that it may overwhelm you with joy. It is that wonderful. Why would you ever want to miss it? And so be it.

Your Brothers and Sisters

WE ARE YOUR COMPANIONS. We come from a constellation you call the Seven Sisters. It is true that we look like you. Genetically we are similar, although our twelve strands of DNA are activated. It is also true that we are blond with blue eyes. It is part of our racial attribute, if you wish to call it a race. We have been facilitating your race for eons. You are us and we are you. We seeded your gene on the planet and watched you as you grew. We are very proud of you and proud to be your brothers and sisters.

We operate in the subtle realm, although we can manifest ourselves if we wish to. Not all of us can, but those who are on missions assisting other planets are masters of energy shifting. We can travel great distances just by changing our energy density. We have mastered ascension, and it is time for us to assist you in moving yourselves and the planet to the vibration that will propel you to shift dimensions. It is a grand process.

As we are you, we know what you are going through inside out. We understand your biology, we understand your psychology, and we understand your physiology. Many of us came in a body just to be part of this final stage.

Many of those you call the indigos are our people being born to your mothers. You see, there is no difference between us except that those who came from our planet as indigos know why they came at this time. They agreed to remember their task and they are different in some aspects. Most of them have biases against violence, against hurting others, against control, against hurting the planet. Some of us are like children: We love to play, laugh, and have fun. You will see that the new children are slow to mature; it is our attribute.

We come in a body because we want to be present when the shift takes place. Some of us know that the ascension of the planet is a probability and not a certainty, but we also know its grandeur.

Some of you ask, *How do we tell who is from another planet and who is from earth?* It is humorous to us that you are still in the dark in that regard. All of you came from other places. You were around long before this planet was alive and you will be around long after it has vanished. You are eternal.

What you have done for the planet is part of what you do. You did it before and you will do it after. We have been doing that with you for a long time. Some of you are us and some of us are you. It is by agreement that you take a life-form and walk in duality. It is by agreement that after your mission ends, you come back to absorb what you have learnt and you continue on your journey. You have options and you do not have to come back to your planet. But then again, why won't you? This life is so beautiful and precious and as exciting as the universe gets. When you are back home, you are with us—looking, observing, and teaching if you choose to.

We have a vested interest in your planet because we are your ancestors. There will be a day when we will appear to you in our physical form and you will see that we are just like you. We have been through wars. We, however, have graduated from that vibration, and we rest and work in a vibration of love. It is a vibration that you may define as bliss. There is no conflict and the feeling of joy is constant. There are fluctuations and there are those who vibrate at higher frequencies and those who vibrate at lower ones, as in your world, but the differences are not as great.

We know that you want to know about us. If you wish to know about us, look inside yourself. We are the same. Our message comes from experience. We have been with you when you moved from one vibration to the next. We celebrated this shift and many of us have dashed to stand in line so we could be born in time to be with you when you graduate. Do you wonder why the earth birth rate is so intense? Many of the newborn babies are coming from our planet. Everyone wants to be at this party.

As we watch you, we are prohibited from interfering with your lesson. It will not speed up your evolution if the learning is not internalized and the transformation is not genuine. You see, it is in the color, geometric shape, and vibration that each and every one of you emits that the planet ascends. If we had given you the correct answer so you could pass your tests it would show in your colors and geometry that you indeed did not internalize the process. We therefore must be careful on how much and when to assist.

This test is about you and you. You cannot fool yourselves, so the teaching is such that it supports you on the journey of transformation.

We wish to congratulate you for being on this planet at this time. There are many who wait in line to be born to your mothers. We love you because we love ourselves. We had to learn to love ourselves first. This is your mission as well.

The most important step in moving to a higher frequency is self-love. It is not what you call being egocentric. Self-love is void of ego. It is the profound understanding that you are one with the universe and you are made of the essence of love. It is the understanding that all life is connected by invisible strings, and when you hurt other life you are in actuality hurting your self. This harmfulness is, by definition, the disease you call cancer. This disease is an attribute of self-hatred manifested in your body. When you are not honoring and loving your body, you create disharmony, which manifests imbalance. That imbalance creates cancer cells that work against the body. On a macro-level, it is what you do to your planet. Your planet is part of you. You and the planet are one. When you do not love the planet, it is because you have not mastered self-love.

The imbalance of the planet manifests in viruses and bacteria. It also manifests in food that has no love essence in it, which actually causes your body to create allergies. It also manifests in destructive forces of nature that attempt to preserve the balance by purging and cleansing parts of itself. It is the same with your body. Cancer is the attribute of a disconnection between you and you. When you understand that you are part of God and you are part of all creation, you have no choice but to love yourself. When you do, you love all life and all creation. When you love all creation, you do not kill and you do not hurt others, because you know that all you do is hurting yourself. It is profound.

Self-love has a biological attribute. It is in the pineal gland. As you evolve, your pineal grows and you develop the capacity to see yourself as part of all creation. You breach the dimension you are in and are able to perceive other dimensions as well.

As you walk on earth in your biology, you feel that you stand alone as a self-sustained form of life, but from where we stand, you are connected by invisible strands to all life. As you act, you change the fabric of all that is. This is your power. When the hordes of entities come from all over the universe to see you it is because what you do affects them as well.

We wish you to understand that all the answers to all your questions are inside of you and if you exercise love in all of your choices, your vibration will change rapidly and you will become that which you are: an angel in plain clothes, carrying the essence of love and changing the vibration of this planet. This is your mission. It is why you came here. We wish you to honor yourself, honor what you eat, honor your fellow man and woman, honor your animals, honor the dirt that you walk on, honor the air that you breath, honor the water that you drink, because all of it is you. And so be it.

Orgasm as a State of Being

*D*O YOU FEEL THE LOVE inside of you? When you look inside, what is it that you see? There are those who search for others so they can discover the love inside of themselves. They look for those people who can mirror for them their own reflection. When what they see is not pretty, they replace the mirror with a different mirror. It is an attribute of a mirror to reflect the self. The same holds for relationships. The one you choose mirrors you. It is not always as pretty as you would like to believe. Many of you choose to skip from one relationship to another, hoping to find the mirror that will reflect you in the best light. We wish to tell you that some of the mirrors, indeed, are polished in such a way so as to expose different parts of you, but the fact remains that all relationships act as mirrors: you of your partner and your partner of you.

We have formed different relationships than you have, because we exist in a subtler form. *What kind of relationship is that?*, you may ask. We are connected through love all the time with our partners. The issues that do come up are resolved energetically through singing and dancing. We also utilize music to harmonize our vibrations. We spend most of our time in what you call a state of bliss. It is a state of knowing the love of spirit and being connected to it. It is what we ask you to discover. All your relationships are mirrors for you. They show you the different facets of your own being. It is not the mirror that you need to work on or replace, but it is you that you need to polish.

You are a sexual being. It is your gift. This gift has been wrapped in ugly gift wrap by many of your institutions. This energy holds the key to your evolution. When you evolve, you do not need institutions because you are free and powerful. Institutions hold the energy of limitations and control. It is through anchors of shame, guilt, and fear that they control your frequencies, not allowing you to climb the spiral of energy that some called the Kundalini. We exist in vibration of orgasm. Orgasm is not limited to your genitals, but it is a certain vibration that resonates with higher dimensions. **Through orgasm you reach into hyperspace for a moment and you experience the melting of all the yous into one. It is as if all of the yous that are playing their part have been spiraled into one vessel. It is from our perspective the highest vibration you can reach with your current awareness. It is why we love you and urge you to make peace with yourself and make peace with your body—to love yourself and honor your body, so you and your body can co-create the spiral of ascension.**

It is our responsibility to impart to you that you must learn how to use your sexual energy in its purest form. Every blemish that you carry in your life as anger, resentment, jealousy, and self-degradation is amplified when it is mixed with sexual energy. When you bring heaviness into sexual relationships, the heaviness will be amplified. When you bring anger into sexual relationships, it will be amplified. When you bring love into a sexual relationship, it will be amplified. Your sexual energy is like the detonator of an explosive. It elevates all the aspects of your inner beings and expels them outward. When you are allowed to use this energy freely and with pure intent, you are free and powerful to manifest what it is that you wish, with ease.

Your institutions know of this energy and are afraid of it. Those who controlled resources on earth knew of the intensity of the power of sexual energy and worked hard to hide it from you and to blemish it so you will be afraid to use it. They were very successful in their efforts, and they created a society removed from the original intention of sexuality. It was diverted and reprogrammed so it reflects power, greed, consumption, fear, and violence— all aspects of energy that when channeled can be used to control you and limit you.

We love you and we wish you to be free. It is your task to clear yourself from all negative feeling related to your body. It is not an easy task, as your cells carry the memory of lives where you were prosecuted for your sexual freedom. What you call STDs are your cells' expressed memory of the pain that you experienced in other lives relating to your sexuality. We wish you to be free from any negativity when you utilize the most powerful energy that you possess as a human. When we hold your hand, we would like to ask you to use all your tools in your possession and not to keep some in your tool shed because they carry the negative energy of the past.

As sexual energy is potent, all aspects of it will be amplified. It is as if you go through a vortex of enhancement, where your cells generate tenfold the energy that they had previously. It is why you must use this energy with pure intent and with caution. Those with whom you interact sexually are your most revered guides. You must honor them and honor yourself. If you use sexuality for revenge or in anger, it will amplify in you and create that which you intended, but inwardly. Your anger will be amplified inside of you because it went through that filter. We wish to tell you that when you come together with another human and you carry the vibration of love and you meld your sexual energies, you leap to other dimensions and create music that resounds in heaven.

Your body is like a string. *Why a string?*, you may ask. Like a string, it vibrates all the time and it sends a certain frequency that, from our perspective, translates into a combination of geometric shapes, colors, and sounds. When you use your sexual energy, it is as if you placed a microphone and a huge screen on stage, projecting your image and sound. Your vibration, whether with light or dark, is amplified. The dark uses sexuality because it knows that it can leverage this energy to spread more darkness. It is your free choice and it is honored as well.

Our intention, however, is to work with light, as we are light beings like you. Our intent is to teach you to ignite your flame and to transform the darkness by using the tools of self-awareness. The one you mix your energy with must be of energy that matches yours in awareness and vibration. When you mix your energy with one that is of less awareness, you place limitation on your own sexual frequency and you may absorb negative attributes inherited from the other person's lack of awareness. One of the greatest challenges now facing your planet is to transform the way you express your sexual energy. It is currently used by those who wish to operate in the shade as a tool to limit your frequency. This energy is utilized to create control, to gain power, and to channel negative emotions. As you are evolving, you must use discernment in your mixing. You must honor yourself first before you mix with another. You may hug yourself first and make a ceremony around mixing with another. We wish you to use your toolbox of intent and say to your body that you wish it to vibrate higher using the sexual energy. You wish it to rejuvenate your cells and allow you to connect to the strings of the universal love energy as you mix. As you set intent when using your sexuality with another, you are using a safety net that allows you to break free from the negativity of your cells and reprogram your body to honor the process and take full benefit from it. It is in the intention that you change the context of your sexual mixing, thus catapulting it into higher vibration.

The orgasm that you feel in your genitals does not begin to tell the story of this vibration. Orgasm is meant to be experienced by the whole body. **You have been programmed to limit this vibration to your genitals, thereby reducing the power of it to mere seconds. The orgasm is a state of being. It is a vibration that your cells were meant to experience for a prolonged period of time. You are enabled to carry this vibration as you walk on your street and we can assure you that you will be smiling.** It is the ultimate vibration of bliss that you are able to carry on your planet at this time. By learning to direct this energy from your genitals to your higher energy centers and coil it up your spine, you begin to teach your body to carry this vibration not only in your genitals, but all over. The more you teach yourselves to use this energy in its highest form and direct it upward, the longer you may experience it. Do you see human civilizations that walk in the vibration of orgasm conducting wars? This vibration, when carried by enough humans, can tilt the vibration of the planet toward peace on earth. It is the highest vibration that you can carry and through which you can connect to your inter-dimensional group. It is apparent to us that so many of you seek sex, but when you find it you become frustrated and angry because on some level it does not meet your expectation. We know who you are. We are your brothers and sisters. It is in your cell memory that you carry the knowledge of the orgasmic vibration, and when the orgasmic pleasure dissipates in a few short seconds you are left with the feeling that there is more to it. When enough of you master the energy of walking in a state of orgasm, it will affect all of life and bring balance to the planet. Earth that is vibrating with orgasmic frequency would not use violence and it would honor itself.

You are your own greatest enemy and your own greatest friend. It is up to you to choose light or darkness. When you mix your choice with sexual energy, you enhance that light or darkness a hundred-fold. This is a great responsibility in a time of the biggest shift this planet has seen since humans have walked on it.

There are those who teach you to avoid using sexual energy altogether. If you are at a place of anger, resentment, and negativity, we ask you to learn to love yourself before you mix your sexual energy with another. However, to avoid this energy altogether is to limit your transformative power from a rocket ship to riding a camel. The keys to transforming yourself are hidden in two drawers. The first drawer is the drawer of self-love. When you open it, you first must see what is hiding inside and clear it so you become aware of what is in your possession. The second key opens the drawer of intent. Your intent acts as the spray that purifies the items that smell bad in the first drawer. Before you mix with someone, celebrate by offering the ritual of intent to yourself and to your partner. Sexual energy is the part of you connected to all the yous, to all your past lives, and to your higher self, and when you mix it with your partner, it is as if you are using a huge mirror to examine yourself. Everything you experience will be enlarged.

We ask you to use caution when you choose to use sexual energy: examine your motives, center yourself, purify your aura, ground yourself, and ask for the highest outcome. Create a ritual in which you invite the highest vibration into your being. Honor the Goddess energy and allow you to channel through you the universal energy of love while engaging with another. Give intent to be an instrument to transforming this planet by celebrating the most powerful tool in your possession, your sexual energy. Honor it at all times, honor those who mix with you, and never use it with negative intent. Use feeling to decipher between those who will allow you to achieve higher vibration and those who will limit your vibration. It is your choice. It is when you honor the process and set pure intent that you honor yourself and transform the earth that you walk on. And so be it.

The Race

L OVE IS ALL AROUND YOU. *What do you mean by that?*, some may ask. *All we see is hate, anger, chaos. Where is the love hiding?* It is hiding in your veins. It is who you are. You think that you are flesh and bones, walking in clothes on your streets, day in and day out. This is not who you are. It is just your outfit. You are made of the essence of love. It is in your cells. Each and every one of your cells is biased to the energy we call love. It is part of your biology. Some of you may consider love as an abstract term that is spiritual or esoteric, but love is an energy that is in your DNA.

When you activate the vibration of love, you send a message to your organs, to your cells, and to your glands that you are ready to move higher in your vibration. Your cells come equipped with all you need to become the essence of love. It is part of your biology. The difference is that as the planet's magnetic fields change, you are asked more than ever before to discover your true identity and activate those cells. Once activated, those cells vibrate at a higher frequency and link you via a certain frequency to all that is. You may call this frequency a melody, because it is harmonic and beautiful. It connects you with you. When your cells are singing the tune of love, you become the one that carries the energy of God in you. What it means is that you are fully connected to your other yous that are part of God, which is also part of all that is. As you walk hand in hand with your higher self, there is no melody more divine than that of the one who walks with his or her cells activated.

At times you feel that you are living in a race of sorts for time. In order to win the race, you must achieve those things that your culture tells you that you should have. It is when you achieve all that you have been sold on, that you discover the real story. You discover that you are no better than you were before you had all these things. The difference is that you have wasted so much energy and the best years of your life chasing after those things that supposedly bring you all you were looking for. From our perspective, what you are looking for is so close to you that it is actually walking with you every day of your life. You travel far to search for something that is so close. It is inside of you, waiting to be activated. We wish sometimes that you could stop just for a moment and join us. We feel that looking at yourself from above may change all your priorities in an instant. We look at you, and we are in love with you. We see you laugh, and we see you cry. We are never too far. We see you lose loved ones and embrace new ones. We see you going through the upheaval of your life and we are with you all that time, waiting for one thing. We are waiting for you to slow down from your "race" enough so you can turn your gaze inward and give the intention to find what is hidden inside of you. As long as you search outside of yourself, no matter how much material wealth you accumulate and how many things, people, or power you gather around you, your light will not be powerful and the earth will not shake when you walk on it. It is your activated cells that change the vibration of Gaia; it is the awareness of your essence that links you to the universe and expands your aura beyond planetary borders.

Your story is much vaster than the one you have been sold on. You came here to transform your planet and the universe, and instead you spend your energy trying to live up to an image that is based on what you wear, where you work, how you look, and how much you make. Does that sound divine to you? Do you think that such a glorious angel, a light being that is eternal and powerful, fulfills its mission by looking good with a set of designer shoes, a fancy university degree, or a fancy job title?

It is wonderful to have designer shoes, it is wonderful to have a university degree or a great job, but this is just the starting point for your real mission. *What is it then?*, you may ask. Your mission is to use love in all that you do, act, and think. It is the activation of the highest potential of your biology. Your mission is to be an activated angel. When you are activated, no matter what you have, what you wear, and how much money you make, you are glowing like a star in the dark night. You are it, and you are fulfilling your mission. You are never judged and always loved. Even those who chase their whole life after the pursuit of happiness wrapped in material wealth and things are never judged. We hug them as well and we try at times to whisper in their ears to look somewhere else, because their treasure is not hidden in their bank accounts.

Although your truth is in you, it is hidden from you. Imagine a horse walking with blinds covering the sides of its head. It can only have a view of the road ahead and that road has no grass. However, on the side of that road there is a lush meadow with delicious grass. As the horse walks the path, it believes that that is all there is and it must rely on its owner to give it sustenance. The blinders that you wear are the ones you accept from your culture. Unlike the horse you have a choice. You do not have to "buy" into the ideas that your culture is selling you on. You promised to come here at this time and discover the divinity within and become an activated human. The frequencies that you take on from your culture are mostly the ones that tell you what kind of a person you need to be so you will be liked, loved, accepted, respected, and supported.

Now what if you tapped into your own cells and discovered that all the respect, honor, and love is inside of you and you did not need any approval from anyone else to walk the path, how would it make you feel? *I do not believe it*, many will say. *We are social beings. Do you want us to just leave everything and be just on our own?* No, dear human, we want you to be the light to your society and culture rather than to be one more victim chasing after that which is futile. As you tap into your own resource, your abundance grows, your health issues clear up, you emit vibrations of joy, and you make those around you vibrate higher. It is by looking inside for the answers and asking your higher wisdom to show you the path that your reality begins to shift. As you set your intent one action at a time, one thought at a time and one breath at a time, you are activating your cells and becoming inter-dimensional. From that place you manifest with ease and you create peaceful vibrations wherever you go. People just want to hug you for no reason, because they just feel like it. Your biology is enhanced and that disease that was scheduled to awaken you is no longer needed, because you have awakened, so it disappears forever. Your cells, operating from a place of joy, are functioning at their optimum level, supporting your biology to function better and live longer. We are your brothers and sisters, and we live in the vibration that you call love. Our cells are activated and all our DNA strands are activated as well. We wish to give you our hands so you can cross that bridge of ascension, allowing your biology and the planet to move beyond the current dimension to a reality that no one predicted or expected. We celebrate each and every one of you and we love you dearly and so be it.

I Want to Go Back

WE WISH TO TELL YOU that you are loved. We wish to tell you that although you do not see the destination of your journey, it is grand, indeed. Yes, we can see it. It is in your potential, and it is glowing with fireworks. *When will we get there?*, you may ask. It is up to you. The timing depends on humanity's collective vibrations. *How do you know we will get there?*, you may ask. We see your direction, and we see your potentials; we see your intent, and we see your resolve, and from where we sit it looks promising. *Are we guaranteed to get there?*, some may ask. You are on your way because you chose to change your path and reach a vibration that prompted the biggest shift you have ever been through. If you all change your mind, well, then it may change your destination, but we do not see that. Why would you want to change it? It is within your reach.

You are vibrating instruments. To yourselves, you appear solid, but to us you are a vibration. We see you in terms of your colors, we see you in term of your light, we see you in terms of the shapes that surround you, and we can hear your melody. You are a giant orchestra and pyro-

technic display, combined. You are beautiful to us; you are magnificent in every way.

Yet many of you look at the mirror and hate what you see. Seeing a wrinkle destroys your day. Seeing a grey hair makes you feel old. You compare your face to the one staring at you from the fashion magazines and ask, *what did I do wrong to deserve such a face, or such a body? Probably it is bad karma.*

We are looking at you from the mirror side, and we tell you that you are beautiful. We ask you to look beyond your skin, as it is so temporary. You are eternal. **You come and go and each time you choose the most appropriate costume to fit your lesson. There are no mistakes. You put great effort into choosing the right outfit. Way more effort goes into choosing your body than all the time you have been choosing clothes to fit your body.** It is a grand process and we wish to talk about that process. After your latest cycle ends you come home. After the celebration in your honor you may choose to stay and work from the other side or you may choose to go back for yet another round. You begin by saying, "I want to go back," and most of you do. First, you come into the circle so you can review your lessons and see what was accomplished and what needed work. You then meet with your teachers and set your goals. Afterward, the process of choosing a body begins.

You need to make many choices.

How about the country where you wish to be born? Is there war there? What kinds of people occupy that land? Will it be a friendly environment to support your path of learning? Well, if part of your lesson, for example, is to learn to appreciate things, maybe there was a life in which you lived very lavishly and wasted much, and later you needed to balance that energy. How about a poor country, or better yet, a rich country but a poor family?

You see there are many considerations. Now, who within your soul group will accompany you? You need a father and a mother, maybe sisters and brothers so your lesson will be richer. It may be that your brother was your enemy in previous cycles, and you died at his hands. Can you imagine that? Yes, there was karma, and it needed to be balanced with love. You both sat down afterward, and you decided that it was appropriate to come as two brothers and to try to work it out differently this time. You set up challenges along the way: maybe a challenge around the family, where a wife of one brother will fall in love with the other brother. Yes, that one who volunteered to be the wife was also in your soul group for a different lesson. She needed to learn about loving herself and respecting herself. She chose to facilitate your karma while you facilitate hers.

Complicated, you say? This is just the beginning. How about a friend who in your darkest hour will give you advice just when you need it? You know who that will be. He was your grandfather in a past cycle, and you had a very special relationship with him. When the whole family deserted him because he was becoming demented, you stayed with him until the end, holding his hand. In this coming life he will be returning a favor. Do you see the magnificence of this system? Do you see the love that goes into the planning? How about the daughter who will be born to you? You know who volunteered to become your daughter? Yes, it is your mother from many cycles ago and, yes, there was something to settle. Many expressions ago, she was abusive, she was harsh on you, and now she wants to experience the other side of the coin. She will be the vulnerable one and you will be the one with a temper and maybe an alcohol problem. Yes, you will need to find peace with all that. Yes, your child will be problematic, and you will be angry often, and then things will happen by appointment and you will have an opportunity to bridge the anger and to find the string of love and to transform hate into love, anger into peace. This is the path of light and all of it by free will and choice.

Have you had enough or do you want to hear more? How about the color of your skin? Yes, you wish to be a black man. *Why would I want that?*, you may ask. *I do not want to be discriminated against because of my color.* Well, you selected it because you were in a place 300 years ago in which you mistreated people of color. You now choose to be in a place in which you will be mistreated so you will understand the other side of the coin. That is how you learn. You explore the energy of being a human from all possible angles.

Now, do you think that all these people who will play a part in your life do not have their own lesson? Do you see the magnificence of the energy you call spirit? All of you, when interacting in life, will have your own appropriate lesson, precise and divine.

Do you understand the sheer magnitude of the planning that goes into each life? That is your path as a human. You are scientists. You are creators, you are inventors, and you are alchemists. Your mission is to turn lead to gold. Your mission is to see all the different perspectives and to come to peace with all of them. Grand enough for you? Then you have others in your life, maybe your future spouse? Do you want to know who volunteered for this mission? Yes, it would be someone that you hurt deeply in one of your past lives. You left her when she was vulnerable. She was devastated, and she ended her life early because of you. Now you volunteered to be with her so she could have another take and find a more appropriate solution, one that involves self-love and trust. Yes, there will be a time in which she will consider ending her life, but then she will have a choice. She can utilize her inner powers and transform that pain to light. She can have again the option to end her life. She chose you to help her, and you said yes. There will be others who will come, right when she will be at her lowest ebb, to help her pull through. One of them will be her angel guide dressed up as her best friend. There is a beautiful contract that you both signed with letters in gold and the contract said, "We will help each other grow, and learn the lesson of self-love, find divinity, and understand our mission."

Your lessons will not be easy and at times will not be pretty, but oh! the potential for light and healing is so grand that you can light a whole town with this lesson. Do you see what goes into the planning? All lessons were created with love and it is all about helping you find the love in your heart, find peace with what was once tremulous, and transform sadness to joy.

This is your journey, and all that time you look at the mirror and say, I am not beautiful and I am not loved. We want to tell you that you are the most beautiful thing in the universe and you are so loved, and so be it.

You Are Transparent

I T I S V I B R A T I O N that we wish to speak about. Vibration is how you and we are connected. It is how you are connected with your other yous. Vibration is your telephone. It is the way you communicate with the universe. It is not what you say that registers with us and with the universe. *What do you mean?* you may ask. *Do our words have no meaning?* Your words are vibration as well, but the meaning behind your words is what we perceive. If you say yes, and you mean no, we perceive the vibration of the no. You cannot lie with vibration. We do not need a lie detector because we see your meaning and not your words. That is why you are transparent to us.

When we tell you that we know who you are, and we know what it is that you thinking about, it is not because we eavesdrop when you pray. We see your wishes, your dreams, your desires, your secret fantasies, your lightest personal jokes, and your darkest ideas. It is all transparent to us because we can see all as vibration. It indeed translates into what we call your music, but it is more than just music. It also has colors, geometry, elegance, and divinity. Your vibration has potential for divinity in every step, and you may go through your life and never find it and never once express that shape, color, and music, but it is there waiting to be expressed. You are a Stradivarius violin waiting for the master to pick it up and touch those strings. We are your brothers and your sisters; where we come from, all are transparent. There is no hiding, and there is no duality.

What is it that you are trying to tell us? Are you saying that we are not truthful? We love you, and we see your divinity, and we know what you are capable of. We can see your thoughts. We know who you are, and we never judge you. It is humorous to us that some of you who play the game of spirituality are intending to play the game of power, and you think that no one noticed. We wish to tell you that your intent reflects all over your vibration. The vibration of ego is very different than the one of love.

Some of you, however, try to satisfy everyone and be gentle and loving, but all we see is frustration and anger. We know who you are and we never judge you. We ask that you do not judge yourself. We hear you at times saying to yourself words of appreciation and we see the vibration of self-degradation. It is the vibration you send that brings light and transforms darkness. You can be the best writer or actor or speaker, but to us, we cannot read the words, nor can we see the acting, nor can we admire the speech; we see what is behind those sensual attributes. We see intent, and we see the vibration that comes in the spaces between the words. If you say the word *love* to water, but it is spoken by a human full of anger, the water will not crystallize based on the word, but based on the intent. Try it.

When you communicate with one another, you still depend upon the words that are spoken or read or the actions of that person. This is now changing. There are already many of you who can feel that vibration of lie, of deceit, of manipulation. Ask your children; they carry extra-sensory ability to detect manipulation. The so-called indigo children know when you are trying to tell them something that is not true. They can feel it in their body. Many of them do not understand that feeling, but they know that something is wrong. This is your new energy, and it will be more and more apparent as you evolve.

The reason we ask you to turn off your instruments of communication, such as TV, is because it reduces your subtle abilities to feel vibrations. Many of your media outlets scramble your frequencies. When you develop that extra ability, the spoken words will not matter as much as what it feels like in your body. How does it vibrate? Does it vibrate truth or love? Does it vibrate fear or anger? Does your body feel one way, while the spoken word vibrates differently? That discrepancy may mean that you are not hearing the truth. **It is the mastery of communication that will change the way you talk to one another. We see it between couples. One speaks one thing, and the other hears something completely different. It is because one speaks words and the other "hears" the vibrations.**

There are those of you who may say, *we want to know how to tell truth from lie. Can you tell us how to do so?* You are doing so every day, but you are not listening to what it is you are feeling. You are all angels who continuously vibrate messages to your cells, to your higher selves, and to your guides. Through vibration you are connected to spirit and to the universe. Everybody in the universe knows your name because they recognize your frequency. It is time now to pay attention to the vibration of things and not to what they appear like or what they sound like.

Some things may appear in front of you that could fill you with fear. When you are in fear, you do not send light; you feed darkness. It is important to begin to use the other sensor, the one that is called the pineal gland. It is in your other eye, the third eye, and is equipped to tell truth from lie.

The new energy is about integrity, about being and expressing your true divinity. The path of truth to your own self is supported and enabled, but the path of hiding your truth from yourself—for the sake of satisfying your fear of rejection, your fear of culture, your fear of anger of others—is no longer possible. You see, others will "see" your true vibration and you will not be able to get away with saying one word and meaning another.

Things are changing, and you need to become one with you. When your vibration is split from your expression, when you do one thing but mean another, you cause splitting in yourself. You send the message of splitting to your cells, and they respond to your vibration and express it as disease.

We love you so and we wish you to prepare, because you are coming into an uncharted territory. You are stepping into the land of mastery. It is your mission to become one with you. It is your mission to hold such a vibration and become sensitive to a degree that you will see the subtle, like the signs you see when you drive on your highways. It is your task to have your inner guides respond to vibration and not listen to words. **There will be a time, not in the far future, when you may be tested. You will be shown a frequency meant to freeze you and send you to hide your light in the corner. It is then that you will need to use all of your power of discretion to separate truth from falsehood not based on the reports from the news, but on the reports from between your eyebrows.**

Are you telling us that something scary is coming?, some of you may ask. We say to you, only if you give it permission to scare you. Your light is needed more than ever, because the dark wants to stay. It knows that the surest way to stay longer is to blow the wind of fear so the candlelight will be extinguished. If you place around the candle a glass lantern of discretion, the dark will not be able to take hold. The old uses fear and the new uses love. Whenever you are in a situation in which things appear to be dark, connect to your heart and pull out the lantern of love and hold it upright and nothing will touch you, as you are so loved and you are so powerful. Do not let anyone tell you differently. When you hold your light, there is no power that can defeat you. We ask you to look for the vibration of anything that is coming to you. Exercise it with your partners, friends, and co-workers, because they are your teachers. When you begin to communicate vibration, you are well on your way to bridging your inter-dimensional self and the part of you that is God, and so be it.

Sacred Heritage

You have a body; your body is an instrument. It does things for you. It serves you. At times, as we look at you, we feel that you serve your body instead of asking your body to serve you. Your body is your sacred heritage. It is your most precious gift. Without it, you cannot exercise your lesson on the planet. Some of you are surprised, then, when your body fails you.

Your body is your version of a shrine. It is a shrine made in your honor. It is given to you to honor your spirit. Your body is magnificent, and it holds the signature of spirit all over it. You are built to ascend and fly. You are built for all the spiritual attributes of which we speak. You have all the potentials designed in your cells.

Your body and spirit are connected, so when you neglect to honor your shrine, it does not serve you as well. It is in the act of honoring that your body holds itself to its highest potential. Your body is made to transfer the energy of love through its magnetic fields to the earth.

When you feed your body with negative energy, it disrupts the original intention of your being and it goes against itself. There are those of you who carry the energy of self-hate. You express it through your body by feeding it the wrong substances. We know who you are. Your body knows of your intention. It reflects you. Some of you say, *this is the way I was born. My mother is overweight, my father is overweight, and, therefore, I am overweight.*

You have chosen your genetic make-up so you can work out your lesson, but that is not to say that your genes and body will not respond to your intention. You are so powerful that you can change your body; you can change the afflictions and tendencies that you came with. Some of you may say, *if that were true I would replace my body in a minute,* and we say to you that it is not honoring your body. You tend to look at people in your culture who represent beauty and say to yourself, *I would love myself so much if I could look like them.* We wish to hug you and to let you know that, many of "them" do not like or honor themselves as well. It is not in the outline of the body that the beauty lies. The beauty lies in the realization that you have chosen a divine body to serve you in the best and most appropriate manner for you to learn and grow. Therefore, you must love yourself and your body, as it is here to serve you.

The heart in your body automatically pumps thousands of time a day, everyday that you walk on earth. Your heart does not complain in the morning and tell you that today it will stay in bed and not go to work because it is too tired. It pumps and pumps. Do you know how much energy is required to pump blood to the whole body so the cells can get the oxygen they need to metabolize? We wish to tell you that it is not an easy task. Your heart is a fine and divine piece of equipment. You received it as a divine gift and as a thank you, many of you feed it with artery-clogging food, just to test it, and then you inhale smoke, which increases the burden even more. Your body becomes even more tired, and your heart works even harder, but it still serves you continuously until it cannot any longer and stops. When it falters because it can no longer carry the burden, you say to yourself, *Bad luck! The kind of body I got.* Instead of thanking your body for carrying that entire burden, you dishonor it even more.

We see that many of you take your gift for granted. Many of you do not honor the greatest gift you have in this cycle: the gift to express and to walk as an angel in disguise. You are loved and there is no judgment in spirit. You make choices and all choices are honored, because it is a sacred space you are in, where free will is your sacred right. When your body tells you that it is thirsty, you have a choice. You can give it a liquid that will hurt it but quench your thirst or a pure live liquid that will strengthen and enliven it and quench your thirst. We wish to ask you: What would you choose? Many of you will say, *Of course, we will give it the good stuff.* The one choice will be soda and the other water. It is ironic to us that you tell yourself one thing and you do another. As you sip your sodas and artificial drinks, you believe that you treat your body well. When you honor your body, it serves you and it gives you energy to do the things that you came here to do. Every time you put something in your body that does not honor your biology, you are sending a message to your body of your intentions. When you give it a substance that honors its divinity, the message of honor and self-love is sent to your body and it will serve you with joy. Your cells will sing differently.

Did you know that your cells sing? Yes, they have a tone that can be harmonious or disharmonious. When your cells sing songs out of tune, you may take on cancer as a manifestation of the discord. You are the most evolved species on this planet and yet you are the only one that knowingly and intentionally self-destructs. All other species, when given the choice, will eat the food most appropriate for survival. They are connected to their biology, so their body intuitively knows what will give it energy and what will deplete it. Some of the species that have been removed from nature and are under your care will adopt some of your ways and will eat whatever you give them. Those animals are honoring your choices as well. If you honor your chickens and feed them well, treat them with care and love, their meat will reflect your caring and will support your biology. **When you place the chickens in a darkened room with bad air and no place to move around, inject them with growth hormones, antibiotics, and bad food and still expect them to give you food that will support your biology, you are deluding yourselves. They are just honoring your choice and giving you back what you ask them to give you.** Take the genetically modified corn that you plant in your soil, for example. If you instruct the seeds to self-destruct after one harvest so some of your companies can sell the same seeds again every year, you are not honoring the earth and its divinity. It will be reflected in the food; the same food that poisons itself will do the same in your digestion tract. It is part of honoring free choice. The food that you grow reacts and knows your intention. You think it has no consciousness, but it has. All animals and vegetation are here to serve you and balance the planet. They know you, they know your name, they know your energy, they know if you honor yourself, and they know if you honor them. If you honor them, they will shower you with love, and when you dishonor them, it is as if you do not honor yourself and they will honor your free choice and give you exactly what you asked for. They will give you food with no life energy and no love. They will give you corn that, once eaten, releases poison. They will give you all that you instructed of them, because they love you and they know the rules of this great game. You are the master, you are the creator, and they are here to obey your choice, whether it is light or dark, whether it is informed or uninformed. Their obedience is an attribute of their love for you and their honoring of your path.

You are surrounded with love that supports you in every imaginable way: the air you breathe, the soil under you, and the water you drink. All the elements respond to you and know your name. It is on you to choose light over dark. We love you and we wish your biology to support you as you transform and shift. With depleted life force, you are not able to move forward with ease, and your progress is slower. There is never a judgment. You are honored just for being here as an angel walking on earth disguised as a human, and so be it.

Love It Is Then

I T IS WITH LOVE that we wish to begin. *Oh, love again?*, you may ask. Yes, we answer as we smile. You are all searching for it most of your lives, and you are already tired of talking about it? Love it is, then.

Love is not just a vibration. It is the substance which fills the space in between all vibrations. It is the glue that holds everything together. *Holds what?*, you may ask. It holds your universe and all the other universes. It holds your dimension as well as all infinite numbers of them. It is the force behind all creation, whether it is in your galaxy or on the other side of your universe. **The love force, as we call it, has the power to create suns and stars. It is even in what you call a black hole. It is the context of matter and antimatter. Most importantly to you, it surges in your veins. Your cells, each and every one, carry that thing you call love.**

And you still wonder why everyone on the planet goes gaga about it. You think that love is just between you and others on your planet. That is a very limited definition of love. In essence it is so grand that when you feel love you are connected, in fact, to all that is. That is why you search for it all the time. You know on your cellular level that there is something out there and you miss it. You yearn for it; you dream about it. It is when you feel in love—looking at your baby in the eyes—that you connect for a moment to that love force and you expand to all the universes at once.

It is not the other human or the baby whom you fell in love with that prompted this feeling of connection. Moreover, it is not just hormones, as your doctors and scientists like to think. Through this mechanism you call hormones your glands align you to the frequency of the universal love that elevates you to a place where you connect at once to all there is. **When you are in love, the substance that your glands secrete actually opens a door, which inter-dimensionally is a vortex that connects you to that love force of which you become part. When you are "in love," you are feeling the vibration that is most prevalent in the universe and in creation.**

Some of you say that you feel like you expand when in love.

We love you so because when you are with us you are in love all the time. It is like the air around humans on earth. Love is our natural environment and when you come home, it is your natural environment as well. Many of you experience that sense of connectedness to the universe and that sense of unlimited expansion when you are in love with someone. Then you misunderstand the whole concept and credit that human for making you feel so high. Falling in love is just one of the ways your body directs you to open an inter-dimensional vortex to connect you to the force of love in the universe.

As most of you have experienced in your lives, falling in love is a powerful feeling. When you are in love, you feel connected, you have no worries, and you feel invincible. You laugh a lot and you want to hug everyone. From where we sit, we see many of you searching after that someone who will make you get that feeling all over again. Many of you believe that only if you meet the right one—your soul mate and twin flame—will you find that feeling again. As we hug you and are in love with you all the time, we want to tell you that another human is only one way to connect to the universal love energy. We wish to let you know that numerous ways exist to connect to this energy, and all of you can and do connect without anyone else's help.

How do we do it?, you may ask. Your body is built to be continuously connected to the universal power of love. It is through disconnection from your body that you distance yourself from the entryways to the vortex. Your body is a divine creation. Within it there are secret doors that, when opened, align you with the core of the universal love. When you open that door that feeling floods you and leaves you in awe. When you are connected, you become that person in love. The difference is that you do not need that other person, and this love is not temporary or conditional. You have access to it throughout your cycle. Moreover, as soon as you connect to it, you find that there are many who fall in love with you, because you carry that special frequency that everyone is after.

In history, when you had a master like Jesus walk among people, he walked in that vibration, and when someone got near him, they were hooked because they felt that same love connection. He was the carrier of that frequency, and he created a vortex by which others could feel that connectedness as well. He was not the only one who could do it. It was available to all back then and even more now.

Some of you may say, *you told us how great it feels, but you did not tell us how to open that door. Where is that door anyway?* Our answer to you is that we also did not tell you how to fall in love. You did it all on your own. It was natural. It just happened. Well, the same truth applies. It is natural, and it is in you, and when you feel it, you know it, like you knew when you fell in love. You did not have doubts when you fell for someone for the first time. You knew that something was going on because you became someone else. You could hardly recognize yourself. We want to assure you that you will know when you get that feeling again.

You are alive at a time and place where the barrier that separates you from the other side becomes thinner. At the moment, some of you can reach across the veil and be in that vibration of becoming one with everything. We wish to tell you in all love that this is the most elevated journey as a human—walking in your biology and at the same time connected to all that is. It is then that you bridge your linearity and become expanded. You become an inter-dimensional human. You then have access to universal truths. It is then that you are able to break the barrier of your limited consciousness and move into a higher dimension.

What we are describing is called by some of you ascension. It is glorious, and it is not easy. You have all the tools in you. Your tools are your biology, and to use them correctly you need the power of intent. The journey to connect to the force of love is a journey inside of you. It is a journey that has to do with complete integration of your soul and your body united in a marriage that through harmony, openness, and intent propel you to places that only a few ever visited, the place of ascension. The secret passageways are in your body. We would have loved to give you a formula, but it does not exist; this journey is different for each of you. This journey is what we call the journey of royalty.

As we hold your hands, we wish to tell you that we cannot give you a map, because you already have it; we cannot give you the knowledge, because you already have that as well. It is all inside of you. You came prepared to do it with all the necessary tools. What we can say is that this walk is about intent and staying open; it is about allowing the other side to show you the way, every step of it. That other side is you, or what some of you call your higher selves. It is a journey that will require you to surrender and trust spirit. When you say to yourself, *yes, I want to get to that place*, things begin to change in your life and you must trust and walk without fear.

In your myth, some of those who attempted to walk that path were depicted as the royals who tried to slay the dragon. The dragon represents the dark side, and the leader of the dark side is the ego. The journey involves moving your body to ever higher vibrations where you will not need to experience physical death. Your biology, however, will remain intact. It is the fountain of youth depicted in your mythology. This journey is not for everyone, and there is never a judgment.

Some of you have ascended in previous cycles and moved off the planet without ever experiencing physical death. Some of you are at it for the second time. We know who you are. Your planet is moving to a place where the energy of ascension can be taken by the masses. It is the first time in your history and in your current biology that the energies enable you to move so high. When enough humans take on the journey of ascension, your planet will reach the fulcrum point where balance is achieved and therefore peace on earth. It will be the graduation of earth from one level of vibration to another, and from one lesson to another. It is what the Mayan called the new sun. It is your potential, and it is magnificent. You are in the midst of that energy and we wish to tell you that it is grand. You are so dearly loved and we say to you: have a great journey and so be it.

Dark and Light

I T   I S   T H E   D A R K N E S S we wish to talk about. When we speak of the darkness, we speak of it as an aspect of the light. It is when the light is absent that darkness is created.

Why do we have darkness?, you may ask. It is part of your being and it is time to come to terms and become peaceful with it. When you fear darkness, you obscure your light. Fear is darkness. When you stand up to that which causes you fear and hold your light, then you transform darkness.

Darkness is not represented by the seemingly "bad" things that happen in your life. Those "things" are part of your lesson. They are either karmic setups or the choices you have made to facilitate your own growth. Those actual events in your life that you see as negative, terrible, horrific, and sad are not darkness. It is the response to those events that represent either light or dark.

When you are in darkness, you are removed from the light of divinity that is in you. When this light is hidden, you are not conscious. There are those who walk in biology, and their light is so hidden from them that they could be called unconscious. When we see you from above or below, we see your light whether it is hidden or not. We see where you are and your potential. We see how you react to things in your life. As you react, you create light or obscure light. Most of humanity is somewhere in the shades of grey.

There are some who operate in the dark shades, and there are some who operate in the most luminescent spectrum. You are capable to act in both polarities and you always have a choice. Those who are unconscious are usually unaware of their choices. When those of the dark, who despite their state of low awareness, manage to find their own divinity, much light is created.

Many believe that taking someone's life is the ultimate darkness, but from the perspective of the other side, that is not so. When you leave your body, there is a celebration on our side, because we wish to welcome you home and celebrate your journey. There is an appropriate death and there is the one that creates karma. All killings or murders are known and were in the potentials before you came into a body. In the circle, all your "possible futures" are known to you. Before you descended into a body, you have looked at all the possible outcomes and you knew about the meetings that you may have to keep unless you choose to change them. The system of your coming and going is magnificent in scope and it considers your journey from all past expressions. What was left unbalanced must be balanced either through "re-action" or through spiritual awakening. You always have a choice whether to keep an appointment or not, but first you must wake up and dust off the webs of karma so you can break free.

All souls who committed the most heinous crime knew of their appointments. It is in the synchronicity of events in which one lesson and one karma intersect and manifest to create learning on both sides. Both the victim and the perpetrator in all violent crimes, as arbitrary as they may seem, were there by appointment. Your life planning is precious and sacred. Your journey is followed by many of us who are waiting for you to reach out and ask for guidance.

Do you think then that people would just drop dead and for some reason that was not planned? We say to you that it always is, and the victim can choose not to be a victim. Also the perpetrator can choose not to commit the act. When you come into life, you arrive with an energy stamp that you collect just before you enter. That is the energy of karma. It spells out your journey, and it carries certain signposts throughout your life, including your time of death. Before you came into a body, you knew that you would have an appointment and you knew when and how it would happen. There is no coincidence even in the most "coincidental events." You also knew that if you chose to awaken, you could change all your appointments and avoid them completely.

When we speak of an angel walking in biology on earth disguised as a human who is not aware of her divinity and her potential to change that path that she is on, we speak of darkness. The darkness, therefore, is not in the events that you come to encounter in your life. From our vantage point, the darkness and the potential for the creation of light lie in your response to these events. Light is created when you make peace with the darkness in you and in your life. Light is created when you become balanced with those things that seem to be so heavy that they feel like they can crush you. You must play the game of duality, and one of the rules is that you must honor your life and fight for it. It is part of your biology and you instinctively follow it. There are those who choose to end their lives inappropriately, thereby cutting short their lesson intentionally. This act creates karma that then needs to be balanced. Nevertheless, that was a potential that was known. There is never a judgment and your choices are honored no matter what.

You come and go very quickly. In the journey and in the coming and going you learn and grow. When you come back, you rest, recharge, and you are already asking, *when can I go back?* When you go back home, you are joyful. When you meet with your guides, you immediately want to review the balance of light and darkness in your previous life.

Your first question to your guides is, *how did I do?* You review and assess all the events that created light and you celebrate them. You also review the missed opportunities and you celebrate them as well, promising that next time you will do better. It is all about the sacred journey and you are loved so much whether you created much light or no light. There is never a judgment. It is all about you wanting to learn all aspects of you. You are a piece of God and you want to continue this glorious journey in which you learn to create and transform through lessons. There is an attribute to your journey that we wish to share with you. Throughout your cycles, you cannot unlearn or forget what you already learned. It means that your spiritual level in each cycle of life begins where you left off in the previous life. You do not forget and you do not need to relearn what was learned. It is a beautiful and divine system.

The light and the darkness are both in you. The whole test that you created for yourselves as angels and pieces of God is about this: When given free choice and your divinity is hidden from you, will you create more light or more darkness? The energy that you choose, through your free choice, is then applied to transform the planet and beyond. That experiment is known by all entities in the universe. You are celebrated just for walking the walk and you are loved just the same whether you were in the balance of light or darkness, such is the system that is so grand and so beautiful that you can't wait to come back for another go at it, and so be it.

Get Out of Bed

IT HAS BEEN NOTED in history that those who walk the spiritual path were named light warriors. We are light beings, and we have worked with those so-called light warriors for millennia. Although we are available to facilitate all those who reach out their hand and ask for guidance, we actively wait for those of you who were warriors in your past.

You came at this time to wake up and shine your light. You promised to be the lighthouses when the storm surge gets high. You knew, then, of your responsibility and you knew the risks. All those who act as lighthouses have done it before. There are no first-timers on these shifts. The lighthouses show the way to those in the dark during storms. They shine their light amidst darkness that those who lost their way may get home safely.

Those of you who promised to be here shining your light and did not awaken, we hug you and gently nag you because it is time. There is no more sleeping, because if you stay in bed for a little longer, you may miss the ride of your life. You may be sleeping while the event that you have waited thousands of years for passes you by.

You are warriors and renegades. Some of you will find yourselves in spiritual institutions doing whatever is it that you do. Deep inside you will know that your mission has arrived, and it is time to get out of bed.

There are those who are part of the spiritual establishment who are asleep. We know who you are. Some of you may say, *but we shine our light. We work with people and we help them. Isn't that enough?* We love you and whatever you do is embraced by spirit, but this is not what you signed for. Lighthouses are standing tall by themselves. They are in a place of storms. Naturally, those places are dangerous and treacherous. There are those of you who signed up as lighthouses and decided to be a lighthouse in a place where there is no risk and no storms—somewhere in the middle of a dry land where there is not even water. We wish to tell you that we love you and there is never a judgment, but you carry a light so those in the dark will be able to see it. Those who shine their light in a place where there is already a lot of light have limited effect.

We know who you are and your capabilities. This is the time to get out of bed and to do the things that you fear and to take the risk that will put you at odds with comfort. Yes, many of you are spiritual and you have that memory. You have done it before and you feel comfortable with it. How about this time around? This is the time when the new energy battles the old energy, and every time a lighthouse is not waking up, there are many who may never make it to shore.

Some of you may say, *but we are working within institutions, why is that a problem?* It is not the institutions that are a problem; it is your light that is not getting to those who need it because it is being obscured by the comfort of the institution you are working within. We see you being comfortable, following the rules, and trying to do what is expected of you. Does it seem to you like the kind of place a lighthouse would stand alone battling the storms? You know why you came here at this time. You have signed up for that special mission that only those who have had experience could do. It requires you to wake up and know that you are renegades. You are the one who does not conform. You are the one who searches deeper and looks everywhere so you can guide others. Do not let dogmas and rules keep you from finding you own voice. You are loved whether you wake up or not. We know, however, that when we meet in the end of your cycle the first thing you will ask us is, *how did I do?* Our answer might be, "Well, you slept through the whole thing." We see your potentials and we wish you to choose the highest path, the one you came here for.

We are in love with humanity. We have worked with you light warriors many times before. We know your names. You are the ones assigned to guide the rest to safety.

We wish to tell you that storms will come, as it is part of the shifting of energy. The new replaces the old. When the transition takes place one must leave so the other can move in its place. There will be a lot of movement. It is spiritual and it is appropriate. We wish to tell you how to recognize that you are indeed the one who was assigned a lighthouse.

You will feel inside an excitement and anticipation, but nothing outside will support that feeling. It is the part of you that wants to wake up, feeling the inter-dimensional pull. At the same time, your 3-D reality does not support that feeling. Some of you will become restless. You will feel that you should be somewhere, when in fact you can't remember where. It is your other part, and us, nagging you, "Wake up, wake up." You will feel that you have a great mission in life and you know it deep inside of you, but nothing around you supports that feeling. In fact you may be stuck in a very boring job or doing something that is very simple. When you share it with your friends, they will think that you may have an ego problem. As we hold your hand, we say to you that your mission is so grand and so sacred that your awakening will change the dirt that you walk on. It will change the constellation of the stars above you and it will help shift the consciousness of this planet. Is it big enough?

What do I need to do to awaken?, some may ask. The first thing is to say, I wish to awaken. You know your job. You have done it before. It is in your cellular memory to hold the light up and keep it in face of a storm. Intent is the first step you must take. You must say to yourself, *I know that it is time for me to wake up to my mission, and I am ready.* And then you say, *Dear spirit: Please, let me know what it is that I need to know and what it is that I need to do.* The answer will come quick. When you get the answer and it is given to you through a song in the radio, which was playing right as you were asking the question, do not dismiss it as a coincidence. This is the swarm of DJ angels who worked the night shift anticipating and celebrating your intent. You have so much support and love around you. All we ask you to do is give intent and remain open.

It is you who makes the difference for others. You can be rich or poor, young or old, weak or strong; it does not matter. You are eternal. Your external outline is a role that you have selected for yourself to play this time around. It is only a role. The part that is eternal is the "real" you and you operate through a body on this planet. Now the alarm clock rings.

What do I do next?, you may ask. You give permission for your life to change is our answer. When you discover your mission, with it comes responsibility. When you give intent, everything around you will begin to shift so you can fulfill your sacred contract. Do not resist the change. Embrace it and celebrate it, because it responded to your intent. *Now what?*, you may ask. You know your job. It is in you. When the storms come and everyone runs to all directions, you will know that it is your moment. It is the time to stay balanced and peaceful. It is the time to comfort others, and it is the time to raise your light high so people will see you and follow you. This will be your call to duty, and you will know it so deeply that you whole body will vibrate differently.

As you stand alone in your tower, shining the light so ships with frightened passengers can pass safely, we want you to hug yourself and smile because you are never alone and with you are all the other lighthouses cheering you. Around you are all the angels just waiting to hug you when you need a hug. When you wake up, we are all here with you. You feel the love every time you open yourself to it. **When those things that happen in the world seem scary, know deep inside that you were built for this mission. You are a lighthouse and you are powerful. This is why you came here at this time and no storm can hurt you. This is when you will feel that you are full. You will know that you are in the right place at the right time. There**

will be no more questions. Do you ever want to miss such an honor? As we ring your alarm clock, we give you one more hug and we say to you, "It is time," and so be it.

Heavy or Light

No one ever came back from the other side. It is a myth that is being told by those who do not believe that you are eternal. It is humorous to us, because you are here and on the other side simultaneously. In your 3-D perception, you are singular and you can be only in one place at one time.

We wish to tell you that it is time to expand your idea of who you are. You can be in various places at the same time and each of you communicates with the other yous. It often happens in your sleep. As you dream, you visit the other yous and check on them. You also experience potentials that could have happened or may have already happened with your other parts. Dreams can be confusing because they are closer to our reality than when you are walking in awareness in your day to day. Dreams have no time and they are the closest things you get to experience the reality of the other side. Hours and days can pass in a matter of seconds. At times you believe that you have been dreaming this long complicated dream that lasted for hours when, in fact, you have been dreaming for two to three minutes.

We wish to tell you that there is so much hidden from you. You are walking blindfolded. We can see you, and we can see your potentials. As you walk in your biology, the only way that you can begin to see is by feeling. If you wish to see further you must connect to the other you, which is part of God. The other you knows why certain things are happening in your life, because the other you is the one who designed it. You always have your two pair of eyes blindfolded and then another set of eyes that are your feeling centers. When you see, it is easy for you to reason and explain what it is that you are seeing. Your visual image is analyzed and is sent to the processing center where it fits neatly into the old familiar ideas you have about reality. When you feel, it is much more difficult to explain it. Your vocabulary is limited to the specific experience and what it means. You may feel something, and it is so layered that you yourself are not sure if you experienced anger, jealousy, or resentment. You do know very clearly when something feels light and positive or heavy and negative. More often than not, you are not able to explain the *why* but you can clearly sense the *what*.

As we hug you we wish to tell you that feelings are multidimensional and it is how we communicate among ourselves and with you. Thinking, on the other hand, or using your rational side, is linear and very limited in the way it delivers reality to you. We ask you at this time to use your feeling center because the reality that you experience is shifting rapidly, and there may be sights that you cannot explain but can feel. We ask that you open up your feeling center. It will serve you well. As the new energy becomes stronger and the old ways weaker, more and more of you will rely on your feelings to know what is true. You will not hear your leaders, but you will begin to feel them. More of you are beginning to develop the language that sees through the words. As you rely more and more on your feelings, those who are in power will become more transparent. Their transparency is not necessarily by choice, but because they will be forced to become transparent, by you. You are changing. It is the old versus the new, and the old is represented by words, logic, reasoning, and appearance. The new, however, is represented by feelings, those of integrity, honesty, and transparency.

The balance on earth is shifting from the masculine to the feminine and you all must connect to your feminine side in order to develop and grow. Many in the old system will find the carpet that they stand on being pulled under their feet, and they can no longer claim the same space that they had before. Many of them will find themselves confused. They used to do certain things every year, and it worked like magic and now they find resistance every which way they go. It is the old versus the new. It is here to stay and you asked for it. You, the angel walking in biology, set up the intention to change the energy of the old and to shift your awareness higher than ever before.

You asked to graduate, and we are your tutors. We want you to succeed, because you have worked hard and earned your degree.

How do we know what is it that we are feeling?, you may ask. You will not know what it means, but you will know how it feels. When you step into a car, do you know how the ignition works? Do you know how the combustion works? Are you familiar with the mechanics of your engine? Unless you are an auto mechanic, the answers are likely no. Yet, many of you use a car every day to move to and from work. The car that most of you know little about facilitates your life every day. You do not need to know what it is that you are feeling and why. It is not necessary.

What you do need to develop is the sensitivity to weight.

What do you mean?, some will ask. *So now we need to watch our weight?* We laugh when we tell you that some of you do and some don't, but what we mean is that you need to decipher what feels heavy and what feels light. **It is by the weight of things that you can measure their energy**

and their meaning for you. When something feels heavy, it means that it pulls energy away from you; therefore, it may have a negative implication on your life. When you feel light, it means that you are receiving energy and that is a sign that you are in the positive. We wish you to find ways to lighten the load in your life by choosing those things that give you energy and stay away from those things that pull your energy. It may be that you will feel that a certain event felt heavy and someone else will feel that the same event made them feel light. **Do not judge the others as each one of you is on a different path and, therefore, what you call your "truth" may differ. At times, two angels will use two directly opposite approaches to reach the same treasure. Do not judge your friends, for what is good for them may not be good for you and vice versa.**

We wish you to stay open and to embrace the beauty of your diversity. You are all eternal and you are all angels. There is not a single human on earth who is not an angel.

So why are there so many problems in the world?, you may wonder. It is too often that some of you who find their treasure in one way believe that all will find the same treasure if everyone would just follow your path. Much of your current strife involves people trying to force their belief system, often related to God, onto others. There are those of you who preach about the one truth. There is one truth when you are in 3D and you experience your life in a linear fashion. As you move away from 3D and begin to expand your consciousness, you begin to experience your inter-dimensionality. As you begin to increase your vibration, that linear truth opens up to a circle. No matter which route you take within the circle of creation, you will reach the same destination. It is the idea of the mandala. **From our perspective, truth is not linear or singular. On a spiritual path there are as many truths as there are angels. One of the attributes of the new energy is that you must learn to honor each other's belief systems, traditions, and words. Those traditions are about intent and about you. It does not matter if you use this prayer or that prayer. It does not matter if you chant this mantra or that mantra. It is about you connecting with you.**

Your mission is to connect with that part of yourself that is God. Who is more qualified than you to find the appropriate way to create this connection? We ask you to understand that your consciousness is now expanding and you are beginning to view the world from many different angles. As you ascend in your vibration, you begin to experience the bigger picture. It is a magnificent one and it tells you about you own story. Those who experience this expansion will no longer seek to force others to see things the way they experienced them. It is you who is on a mission to connect with yourself. We love all of you, as we are your brothers and sisters. We wish to whisper in your ears that it is through intent that you find the love of God inside of you and not through any other means. When you do, you embrace all other angels because you know that although all of you arrived wearing different clothes and chanting different prayers and using different colored beads, you all ended up at the same gathering at the circular arena, and it is indeed an awesome sight. We wish to celebrate with you your journey as we are with you every step of the way and you are dearly loved, and so be it.

Wait a Minute

W E ARE HERE AGAIN.   We are very pleased to go through the veil and meet with you. It is such a pleasure to be sequestered. Your intention to move forward is what allows us to connect with you directly.

Those of you who wish to learn how to co-create with spirit should take note, as there is an appropriate way to do so and an inappropriate way. When we speak of inappropriate there is never a judgment. We love you whether you connect with us or not. We do, however, wish to hold your hand through the process, as it has its own mechanics. There are those of you who tell us what you want. You say, *Please give that which I want and I will be grateful.* We tell you that this is not the proper way to ask. When you wish for something, you ask it because it is what you think you need at the moment from your blindfolded, linear perspective. We will honor your request, but you may not thank us in the end. You see only what is in front of you. What is in front of you may not be what you need in order to grow. Often it is to the contrary. That which you wish for may stifle your growth and divert you from your purpose. There are many of you who ask for material wealth. You say in your prayer, *Dear God, if you could give me so much, I will be a better person. I will even give to the poor. I will also be happier and will stop drinking or being angry at my family. I am only angry at my wife and children because I do not have enough. I have to work so hard and I come home tired and stressed out so I yell at them.* We love you and we know who you are and we also know the challenges that you face. Remember that we are with you every day of your life. We wish to impart to you that your vision is limited, so you feel hungry and you immediately ask for food. You say, *Dear God, what I want is a nice big meal all you can eat buffet-style so I can eat as much as I want.* What if instead of showing you the road to get that one meal, we gave you the instructions to create your own buffet-style menu that will go with you wherever you go, so you will never go hungry again? *But I am hungry now,* some of you may say. *We do not care about learning to build our own. It will take too long, and we want to eat now.* That is why we love you so. Do you wish to be hungry tomorrow and what about the day after? You are eternal, you know. If we lead you to this one meal, it will be like giving enough air to a human so she can take one breath. If she wishes to breathe again, she needs to ask for it again. You come and go quickly. Your journey is not about having; it is about learning. You learn how to move from drama to peace or how to move from scarcity to abundance so you never need to worry again.

It is the hunger that propels you to seek those solutions, so you can learn and grow. There are those who are hungry and they find food on someone else's plate and steal it. This is one way to satisfy one's hunger; however, it does not serve your lesson and therefore it is not appropriate. When you ask us for things, you do not fully know how those things will serve your path.

Sometimes, you do not know if those things you are asking for will create turmoil in your life or bring peace. You may not know if those things will create karma or relieve karma. Many of you ask for those things that will add weight to your lives and slow your progress. Many of you are led to believe that bigger is always better and that more of something must be abundance. Again, this perspective is linear.

We wish you to move from the floor and climb to the mountain top. When you reach the top, the view opens and you can see where you need to go. You widen your outlook. A GPS system tells you whether to turn left or right so you will reach your destination. To use a GPS, you need to first know the final destination's address. Most of you ask for the right and left without ever asking for the final address. Then, many of you get lost in taking many lefts and many rights, but you are never moving forward and never getting closer to your final destination. **Often it is the opposite: By asking and receiving that which does not serve your path, you go backward and find that the more you have the less you feel. The more you acquire, the less you have time to enjoy. The more you have, the more separated from your family and people you become. The more you have, the less happy you become. You asked for more and more, and because you are the creator of your reality, that which you ask for will manifest.**

We ask you, then, why would you ask us to have less quality time, to be more stressful, to have less joy, and to be more separated from your loved ones? We wish you to begin asking in a way that will serve your path. We love you and we wish you to move away from those lessons that lead you in circles. It is in the solutions to your karmic setups that you are propelled to move forward. As you move forward, you become lighter, more joyful, more personable and loveable. You become more peaceful and fun to be around. You become healthier and more energetic.

The next time you kneel down before bed and give us your hand, why won't you ask to find the path to your truth and to your divinity? Instead of asking for that brand new car and that raise in salary, ask to be shown the way to have more free time in your life, ask for the mores that are of feelings and not of "things." When you ask for help to find peace in your life, we cry from joy because you speak to us in our language. We understand feelings, we know what peace is and we know who you are. We know of all your potentials and we can direct you there safely.

Next time just sit on the floor and be quiet. Do not even ask for anything. Just trust that we know what you need. Just give yourself a hug and say you love yourself and you know that you will find all the things that serve you because they are all given to you with love. Maybe next time you sit to meditate, just say thank you. We will hug you then and we will celebrate you because you made a leap from your limited dimension to ours.

Some may ask, *how would you know what I need? I have rent to pay and if I do not pay it by next week I may get evicted.* As you are walking blindfolded, you ask for that which will cover the rent for this month. "How about next month?" is our question. What if instead of giving you a solution to pay rent for this month we will lead you to a place where you never have to worry about rent again? *This is not possible!* , many of you will say. *Do you want us to live on the street?* What if we tell you that it is all about helping you create miracles in your life? It is about co-creating magic so the impossible becomes possible. **You are the creator. If you believe that you can only** create something small, that is exactly what you will manifest. How about asking to be shown the way to your highest potential and to your most glorious path and forgo the specifics? How about trusting that the universe knows your highest potential? From our perspective, when you leave the door open, magic takes you by the hand and leads you to where you never imagined you could be. Next time you sit and worry, trust that we know who you are. We know what you need, we know about that rent that needs to be paid. Just trust and ask to be shown the way.

We are in love with you and we wish to tell you that you can only co-create with spirit that which you have intended. When you ask for our hand, know that you will be shown the way, as your higher-self begins to change the plans and to coordinate new plans that will serve your life best and lead you to your highest potential.

When your life changes, do not say, Wait a minute! I just wanted the rent to be paid, but I do not want to change my life for that. When you ask to create peace in your life, when you seek to create abundance in your life, or when you seek to find joy, you must be willing to change so those things standing in the way can be cleared.

As we complete our lesson about how to ask for what you need, we give you one last hug and we whisper in your ears. Just intend to find the divinity inside and follow the path one step at a time. Understand that you will need to agree to change, to stay open and trusting. Fear is your biggest obstacle in finding your treasure. When you move through fear and allow your higher part to be your guide, then magic and miracles will become your reality. You are living in a special time and you are able to co-create miracles every day of your life, and so be it.

The Traffic Jam

WE ARE YOUR BROTHERS AND SISTERS. We sit beside you day in and day out.

When you act in the world, there are those who follow your actions. They follow you wherever you go and wait to put signs before you so you will know whether to turn left and right. They are in love with you and get emotional when you recognize and follow their signs. They have a special language that we wish you to recognize. There's nothing that will make them happier than an awake human walking on earth and following the signs of the brothers and sisters you call guides.

These guides are not separated from you. They are part of you. They are part of your group. They love you and they are with you all the time until you go back home. They are loyal, for they have been with you for a long time. Some, forever. On every cycle you have walked on earth they were with you. You are eternal, as are they. When you walk in your biology, you are a group. Their energies assigned to you are part of your group. They listen to your higher self and try to steer you toward your life plan—the one you planned before you came to this planet. When you sat in the planning room signing contracts and scheduling appointments, they were there with you. They are your entourage.

Why do you tell us about this? you may ask. As you walk in your daily life, we wish you to learn the signs that your entourage is using to speak to you. When you begin to follow their signs, you become the one who walks hand in hand with your higher self.

Imagine that you are a king or a queen with a group whose only care is your well-being. They love you and are loyal to you your whole life. They agreed to devote all their energy and love to you so you could rule your kingdom wisely and make the right decisions. Wouldn't you like to be such a lucky king or queen? Wouldn't you listen to your entourage and consult with them? After all, they are loyal only to you and they have no agenda of their own. They only wish to hold your hand and lead you to your highest potential.

I wish I were that king, some of you may think. *But I am no king and I have no entourage.* We wish to hug you once again and let you know that indeed you are those kings and queens. Indeed there is an entourage walking with you all the time and they love you throughout your lives. You come and go and they are with you. The difference is that they are not in duality. They know who you have been and they know why you came this time. They know of your lessons. They know of your challenges and they know about your appointments. Remember, they were with you when you planned everything. They do those things that are subtle to remind you of your appointments. They operate in a quiet way so you must be in a quiet place to understand their message.

Now it is our turn to ask you a question. If you indeed have such a group, wouldn't you want to get to know them? After all, they know you so well and love you so much. Wouldn't you want to give them a hug or just say thank you? They never ask for that acknowledgment, you know. You can walk in biology your whole life and not even know that they exist. You may not say thank you and at times you may even become angry, for their loving messages may come camouflaged in different costumes. At times it may be in the form of a flat tire or of a phone that does not work. They do those kinds of things.

Why would they be busy with my car or my phone?, you may ask. As we said, they see the potentials. They know that if you did not stop to repair your tire, you may have ended up in that accident that happened down the road exactly at the time you were scheduled to drive by. *What about the phone?*, you may ask. If your signal was working, you would have received a call that your appointment was canceled. What if that appointment was layered with another appointment, one that you made before coming to this planet? What if that appointment was very important, because it was a karmic meeting and you had to be there so you would begin a new path? Because you have not gotten the call, you have waited and waited in the lobby of an office and synchronicity had it that someone approached you and asked you if they could help you. You have begun a conversation and you found out that you had things in common. You exchanged phone numbers.

Advance that day five years and you will see a different picture. You are holding a baby, and the one standing beside you and smiling is the one who asked if she could help you. You think that things just happen. Well, next time we ask that you celebrate that which is seemingly a coincidence, because so much planning goes into it. All day long you are being directed. You call these things accidents or coincidences. You get frustrated when you are stuck in traffic. You curse often when the place that you intended to go to closed just as you arrived. We love you and we know who you are. You are an angel walking blindfolded, thinking that everything around you just happens. Next time, when you are in traffic and your car is not moving, why don't you celebrate it? Celebrate the fact that you are not in that car half a mile ahead that was crushed in a head-on collision.

There is a mechanism that we call "your guides." These guides are your most loyal friends and they are with you from the time that you exit the womb until the time that you breathe your last breath. They see you in your lows and they love you just the same. They see you when you falter and they love you just the same. You call it unconditional love; here we call it the love of spirit. There is never a judgment. You judge yourself, but your entourage never does. The relationship that you develop with your guides is the relationship between you and you. They are part of you. You are a group and they are part of your energetic essence. When you walk on the planet, you have them paving your path so you will keep your appointments. When you choose to vibrate at a higher level, they often have an all-night celebration and you cannot fall asleep because of their excitement. In the morning, as you drag yourself out of bed, you feel hung over, as if you have partied the whole night. Guess what? You have!

You are becoming thinner. Some of you may say, *Oh that is great because I have been trying to lose a few pounds.* We see your energy and to us those pounds appear as density. Those of you who give intent to vibrate higher become less dense. Your body appears to us more transparent and more brilliant. As you move higher, your guides have more access to you. They operate in the subtle realm. As you become subtler, they can communicate with you more easily and show you signs and symbols without needing to orchestrate the more obvious messages. **The mechanics of your guide's messages move from light to heavy and from the subtle to the gross. It is when you do not react to the subtle message that the follow-up is heavier, and so it goes. When you get a painful message, you may want to look back and examine the signs that were there, but you missed them because you were too busy moving around.**

When you open up and create relationships with your guides, then your life takes a divine course. When you embrace that which crosses your path and celebrate it, your life follows a divine course. Many of you walk in darkness, feeling victimized every time your plans do not manifest the way you imagined them. We wish to tell you, with all love, that your plans are very linear. You do not see what is behind the curve, because you can only see that which is in front of you. You have designed this limitation for yourselves. It is through understanding who you are and the divinity of your path that you begin to broach the limitation and develop an inter-dimensional vision. Your guides are your eyesight. They have your best interests in mind. They are you, inter-dimensionally. They are your bridge between the human walking in duality and the unlimited "I am that I am." Next time, hug yourself and acknowledge the divinity of the system you call coincidence. On this side we call it synchronicity and we wish to tell you that it is a sacred system. It is a system where your intent and that of your brother angel and sister angel are being coordinated to serve all of your lessons and growth. Can you imagine the intricacy of such a system? It is a system so complex that it could only be devised by the one who is experiencing it. And that is you.

We know who you are and we know your challenges. Next time you are in a place where things that you did not want happened, and that which you were afraid of manifested, we wish you to hug yourself and celebrate the lesson. Thank your guides for their teachings and guidance. Know that they are stirring you to where you asked to be. You may not see it yet, but trust it because they have the overview. We wish you to move away from the place of victimhood. When you feel like a victim, you blame someone else for that which you yourself created. From where we stand, you are walking in darkness and those lessons that you are given with so much care and love are going unnoticed. You are so loved, yet you think you have been abandoned. When you see yourself as a victim, that lesson you have been given has not been learned nor integrated. Next time we wish you to celebrate that which you find difficult. Thank your guide for devising such a genius program so you will be almost forced to find your light. Celebrate those things which were forced upon you—that phone that has no reception and the traffic jam—and know that you are loved and all that is around you is given to you with a gold signature inscribed *love* on it. We wish you to celebrate it, as there are no coincidences in your life, only opportunities that you asked for and received so you will be able to progress. This system is beautiful and you are beautiful, so celebrate that beauty in your life. In those events in your life that spell *challenge*, we wish you to take a moment to embrace the divinity of that challenge and know that it was given to you with love, and so be it.

A Fish Riding a Bicycle

THERE IS A GREATER STORY OUT THERE. The story is in the circle. You are always searching for answers. Many of the answers are in front of you. Most of you can't see them because you look in straight lines, but the answers are in the circle.

It is the story of the three-dimensional reality versus the multidimensional reality. Explaining multidimensional reality to a human is like explaining to a fish how to ride a bicycle. It is a different reality; so much so, that the only way for us to describe it is through metaphors. Although metaphors do not tell the real story, they convey the feeling.

The first obstacle in bringing our reality closer to you is the barrier of time. In your reality, everything has a before and an after. In your language, you have past, present, and future with each verb. How do we then bring to you something that is so different from the reality that you are accustomed to? *Just tell us how it all began,* you say. *Was there a big bang?* With all love, we must tell you that it never began. It always was. As for the big bang, there were many of them and they did not start anything. The bangs are an integral part of creation, and you were there when it happened. Some of you may say, *that is not possible. That was billions of years ago, and there was no earth and no galaxy before the big bang. How is it possible that we witnessed it?* My dear angels, we told you that you were old, didn't we? *You mean to tell us that we were there when it all began?* Yes, dear humans, and even before it all began. You were here when it was just in the planning phase. *So how long will it last?*, some of you may wonder. *What will be the end of us? Will it be when our sun dies?* You are eternal, dear human. When your sun dies, you will move to a different planet and do what you do. You will take a body and be part of creation through that body in a different part of the universe. *You mean to tell us*, some may ask, *that we will outlast the sun?* Yes, dear human, this sun of yours and many others. You are eternal. We know your limitation. When we say eternal, you look for a beginning and an end. You are built that way. When we say no time, you ask then, *what's next?* That is why we love you so much.

You created a reality unique for you so you could learn about yourself. *Why would I do such a thing?*, some may ask. It is because you collectively are the creator. This is what you do. You learn about energy so you can continue to create and explore that which is you. As you create, you learn about yourself and so the circle grows.

We told you about the circle. You are it. Your lesson on earth is still part of the circle, but you cannot see it. You only see linear lines because you are in the dimension of time. In your dimension there must be a before and an after. In our reality there is a circle and you can get to any part of the circle from where you stand. In the circle there is no time. What was, is, and will be is all there to be viewed. More so, even the potentials that were supposed to happen but did not can be viewed.

Some may say, *you are confusing us. If something happened in the past, it already happened and we understand that you can see it, but how can you see the future?* As we hug you we answer that we see all your potentials. We cannot see which one you will choose. That is your free choice, and it is sacred. No one can tell which future you may choose. All your probabilities exist and we can see them. Some of you may wonder about prophecies. Nostradamus saw what was coming. How did he do it? We tell you with all love that he saw the probability, and he took a guess. It was a good guess, and at times he was correct and at times he was not. He predicted the Armageddon close to the end of the millennium. We wish to tell you that what he saw was a very reasonable probability, and you were on track to fulfill it for many years. We also wish to tell you that you have changed it in the past thirty years. You could have had a planet without people and only plants and animals and you chose to stay. Does it tell you a little about your power?

How useful is that information to us? What should we do with it?, some of you may ask. Know that you are eternal and that you are the creator of that which we call earth lessons. Know that whatever you do, you can undo because you can switch one potential with another, one reality with another, one channel with another.

You are on the eve of a new era. It is you who chose to vibrate higher and change your future. Your future was a probability, and you have chosen a different probability, a truly grand one, and you are on track to graduate. We wish to impart to you that your time, as you know it, is collapsing. You are experiencing an acceleration of time as you know it. What it means is that various dimensions are colliding and you will begin to experience multiple realities simultaneously. It means that it can get very confusing for you unless you develop your extrasensory abilities so you can maneuver yourself.

What will I experience?, you may ask. You are already experiencing a shift in the magnetic fields of the planet. Time as it used to tick for thousands of years is changing now. Your dimension is colliding with other dimensions and we wish you to prepare for sights that you are not used to. You may encounter yourself in your own past from another life. It can be very unnerving, although it doesn't have to be. You may experience all your past lives as they are happening at the present. You see, all the lives that you have ever lived are in that circle that we spoke of. You are still working the land with your mule or rowing your canoe up the stream. It is all there and it is happening simultaneously with the life that you are leading now. We can see your past lives, because in our reality they are happening now. All of the yous in the many forms that you took in all of your existences are in the now. That is why we urge you to learn to be in the now, because the now is truly all you have. Being in the now will prepare you for a reality where the dimensions of time collide and you may find yourself as you were 150 years ago.

We ask you to rely on your feeling and not on your sense, because things will not make sense anymore. As your dimension collides with other dimensions, your brain will not be able to place your experiences into the 3-D box, and you may go into fear, blocking the magnificence of this event. You can choose not to use fear. If your feeling centers are open, you will know that what you see is a shift in consciousness and you will be able to integrate the new reality into your feeling center. You are at a place that no human has entered in your biology since you walked on earth.

The universe is shifting around you, allowing your biology to change so you can integrate your sense of reality with the reality of multi-dimensions. There are those of you who may say, *this is too scary. Where should we hide?* We wish to tell you that your home is getting closer to your earth experience. When you are with us, what we speak of is your reality. As you walk in duality and the biology of a human, all this "truth" is hidden from you. As you get closer to graduating from your test, the once-hidden reality unveils itself. You will begin to experience more of the reality of angels free of duality. You will begin to experience the reality that is behind the veil.

Are you scared of love? Maybe you are scared of peace. Can you tolerate an angelic sense of humor? If love and peace are not scary, maybe you should consider sticking around, because they are coming, if you choose to allow them.

It is a choice and we must tell you that there are those who wish to stay with the reality of the old. They may not experience the shift and collapse of time the way you do. They might experience fear and create a reality very different from the one we are describing. As dimensions collapse into each other, there may be more than one reality on the playing field. One reality can be called heaven, and the other may be called hell. One may experience despair and the other bliss. Both will be on earth in their bodies

in this dimension and both will experience that which they choose. Their experiences, however, will be very different. That is why we urge you to learn to identify your reality based on emotions and to find the subtle. You are at a crossroad, and your feelings steer you to experience that which we call bliss or that which we can define as despair. We urge you to vibrate higher so you can decipher what is happening.

You are about to experience the ride of your life and we are your cheerleaders. We are in love with you and excited about your prospects. We wish you to be prepared so you will know what it is that you are experiencing. We wish you to be ready so you can enjoy this ride. After all, you stood in line to be on earth at this time. You said that you would not miss it for the world. You knew about Armageddon and you still took a body. You have changed your path and you are on the most glorious potential. We love you and we want you to be able to take it all in, and so be it.

The Cell Phone

ONE OF THE WAYS TO DISCOVER the divinity inside is to be in the world.

There are those who say, *let me hide for awhile. Let me be a hermit. When I am by myself, I will find the truth.* We know who you are. There are those of you who wish to hide because each interaction with the people around you brings drama. You say to yourself, *I am sick and tired of people. They are all foolish and unenlightened. Let me seek those who are enlightened or just hang out with the animals.* We see you struggle with your family. We see that you are the only one in your family that seeks to find something behind the day to day. We see that you are tired because those who are called your family or friends do not understand what it is that you want from them. They get frustrated with you because you always ask questions and you do not accept everything that everyone else accepts. Does this sound a little like you?

We know that it is not easy to be an old soul engaged in the new reality amidst younger souls engaged in the old reality. They do not question anything, because they are just

excited to be around. They seem like they are having fun. A nagging feeling, however, weighs on you and keeps you awake at night. You know something profound is going on, so you do not understand how everyone around you sleeps like logs while you twist and turn. You wonder often about your sanity. Sometimes you even hear voices and you are not sure who it is talking to you. You turn to the left and you turn to the right, and there is no one. Then you think to yourself, I hope no one noticed. We love you so much and we walk beside you when you are moving around your family or in your place of business.

You are on a mission and you are tired. You are tired of being the only one. You wonder at times how long it will last!! You ask yourself, *when will I find those like me so I can speak my mind, or if it will ever change?* We wish to tell you that it is changing, dear human. It will change like your communication changed 130 years ago. Back then only a few of you had a telephone in your homes. You all knew each other and you had to connect to each other through an operator. It was not too long ago that you discovered that if you had the mechanism you could connect to those who also had the mechanism. We jump to today and many of you, worldwide, hold a device that is called a cell phone that lets you communicate at any time. What was rare became a household commodity, and almost anyone who can, uses one. It became part of your culture.

You may say, *are you telling me that I have to wait another 130 years to find people like me?* Time is moving rapidly and what took a century to be established now takes a decade. Look at your cellular revolution. You had land phones for several decades before people began to use cell phones. Within a decade, almost everyone uses one. And the reason everyone uses it is because it works to facilitate your lives. It allows you to function better and be more efficient. In fact, those of you who do not have this device stand out. In Western society, many consider it almost indispensable.

Why are you telling us all that? This will be the story of the new energy versus the old energy. You are pioneers and you are at the forefront of the wave. We wish to tell you that the masses will follow soon because it works. It will become obvious that certain spiritual attributes greatly enhance your life. We see the potentials and we wish to tell you that they are glorious.

Some of you may say, *this is not possible because all we get is bad news. Everything around us seems so difficult.* We know who you are. It is part of your contract and you signed on to be at a place where you lead by example and keep your light. As you move around, your light shines until such time that it gets to be a critical mass. Once that happens, the planet will brighten up like a fireworks display. **You think you are the only one, but there are many** of you old souls working the trenches in places where the light is very dim. They are doing what you are doing. They are acting as vessels to channel the frequency that allows the spiritual attributes of the planet to change. You are doing inter-dimensional work by keeping your light on. It is a sacred work and you have a group that watches you and supports you day and night. When you can't sleep at night, they stay awake as well. You are dearly loved and your light is needed.

How long do I have to wait?, you may ask. The short answer is, for eternity. This is what you do. The long answer is, soon enough. This is the battle that you signed on for. You do not wear a uniform and you do not get medals. You walk in your duality and in your biology, shining your light wherever you go. You stay balanced where all around you there is chaos. You keep your inner peace while your partner or spouse is in turmoil. You walk knowing that there is divinity inside of you and those who are around you, walking in darkness and feeling victimized, carry the same divinity that you do. Moreover, you do not need to say a thing to any of them. They are entangled in their drama and you walk in peace, because you know who you are and you know what it is that you came here for and what is your mission.

Why do you think you are the only one in your family who carries spiritual awareness? Did you think maybe that your light would be a catalyst for another member of your family to start searching? It is like the ripple. You are the first drop and the others feel the ever-growing vibration and they begin to ask, *what does she have that I don't? Why is she so radiant? Why does she look loving when everyone around her seems to be in pain? Why does everyone want to be near her?*

We know that you are tired. We wish to tell you that this is your battle. You are in the midst of it. Your mission, as a light warrior, is to hold your light. Your mission is to find peace inside of you despite the turmoil that is all around you. Do you see why you need to be with people and not in the mountains? The mountains do not need your light; other humans need it. This is how you change the planet: one drop at a time. Who do you think will do the job, God? We love you and we wish to tell you that God it is. You are part of the energy you call God, and although it may not be the miraculous fireworks that you may have expected, it is that part of you that is God doing the work to bring light to this planet. You are the messenger of that energy you call God, and you are the one performing magic and transforming darkness into light.

Do you begin to see why you are where you are? You are where you need to be. You are at the right place at the right time, doing what it is you asked for. This is it and it is wondrous. So many of you are waiting for something drastic to happen, like your Hollywood happy ending with the hero saving the heroine at the last moment and riding with her toward the sunset. You are the director as well as the actor of this movie. It may not be as sparkly as the Hollywood production, but on our side of the veil we lay a red carpet for you every time you find your inner peace in the midst of chaos. When you use love to combat anger, we hold celebrations. This is the work. It is about transforming yourself one act at a time, one thought at a time.

You will see that soon there will be more and more who see what you see. The new children already stare at you funny, because they know that you carry their frequency. It is coming and you are at the forefront of that energy. We wish you to be patient and celebrate the moment and celebrate the challenges. Like the cell phone phenomenon, the spiritual energy that is flooding the planet will be self-evident. The planet will support those who aligned with the energy of integrity, feelings, love, and cooperation and will not support those who still use the method of the old energy. The old used masculine rational fear and control-based actions. That is changing and everyday there is more light coming and more darkness transforming. We wish to tell you that you are dearly loved and you are where you need to be, and so be it.

There Has Never Been
a Better Time

THERE HAS NEVER BEEN A BETTER TIME to free yourself from the old and start new. *Why is now better than before?*, some will ask. Time is always spinning.

You are on a journey and many of you are walking on a treadmill. You sweat and you breathe hard, but you get no benefits. Instead of getting in shape, you are just wasting your time. There is no better time to realize that you are eternal and to shed your fears. Once you shed your fears, you begin to flow with the time. As time moves more rapidly, you will slow down. *Why will we slow down if time is moving faster?*, some may ask? Isn't it a paradox? **As time moves faster, you must learn to slow down so you will stay in balance. Your biological clock will be ticking at the same rate, but your perception will be that you are slowing down. It is because everything around you will move faster. We know it is confusing, but you are about to enter a confusing time in which your logical mind will be stretched and challenged.**

This time is the best time to pull inside and take stock of who you are. Regroup and begin a new chapter. It is the year of newness. The energies around you are all about new and rebirth. We ask you in all love not to hold back on your dreams. We salute you when you remove fear from your daily life and do that which makes you vibrate higher. When you are happy, you are literally full of light and the planet needs light. We wish you to find the flame in your life. Many of you fear that if you do follow your dream everything that you built so far will collapse. It indeed will collapse. Do you know what will collapse? Your frustration, your anger, your burdens, your heaviness will collapse into the earth and a new, lighter you will sprout where the heavy fell. Why are you so afraid to let go of that which is heavy in your life?

Many of you fear the feeling of lightness. You fear being happy because you suspect it. If you are happy, something will go wrong and will show you that it was just temporary. Many of you carry memories of times in past cycles when you were happy and then everything changed and the happiness was taken away from you. Many of you hold back on your lives because the thought of experiencing happiness terrifies you. As long as you feel in a slump, you know where you are and feel comfortable with it. Happiness is a new territory to many of you. We are in love with you and we never judge you. If you wish to experience a life of misery, we honor your wishes. It is the lesson you wish to learn and we hold your hand, regardless of the choices you make.

Our question to you is: Why would you choose to be unhappy? Many of you may say, *oh, this is my destiny. I always knew my life would be hell and here I am in hell. I can't wait for it to be over.* The hell you see is inside of you. It is not what is out there; it is what you choose to see. We ask you to consider choosing differently. From where we stand, not one of you was destined to a life of unhappiness. All you see is setups to resolve and move beyond them. There is no situation in your life that is not resolvable. We wish you to remember that you planned all these setups and you also had solutions in mind. For each challenge there was a path that solved the challenge. We ask you not to wait. Time is short, and you are eternal. You come and go, but this time is different. You came at this time because all your long-forgotten abilities are there for you to recall from your akashic records. You can be whatever it is you desire because your access to your own records is enabled.

We wish you to tell yourself that the time is now. There is no tomorrow, only the now. Do not wait for the opportunity in the future. Many of you give yourselves excuses for why it is difficult to move away from heaviness. It is true that gravity pulls you down stronger the heavier you are. We ask you to become lighter so when you laugh, you really

mean it, and when you tell your friends, I am happy, you really mean it. When you find the time to feel, it means that you stepped off the treadmill.

You are eternal. It is a hard concept for you to digest. You come to explore yourself and you come to learn about energy. When you are paralyzed in fear, it is as if you bought a ticket to the merry-go-round, but you looked at it from the side, never to go riding.

There are those who do not want to pursue that which makes them happy, because they are afraid to lose what they already have. Regardless of how little happiness they have, they still hold on to it like a raft in the middle of the ocean.

You have been taught to survive. We ask you to let go of your survival and trust that when you let go of the old, only then you can begin to move in the direction of the new.

You all came with aspirations. Many of you waited in line to be on earth so you could do good. Many of you came with plans how to help humanity in these challenging times and make a difference. We see you and we know who you are. We also see those who remain like children. We also see those who wake up in the morning and cannot wait for the day to begin. We see those who are so excited that they sing in the shower and when they walk to work or home. When you are happy, you glow from the distance. When you look up in a clear sky and it is night and you are somewhere in nature, you can see all these stars and they are all sparkling. Now when you stay gazing at the stars, some seem so much brighter than others and they begin to wink at you. This is how we experience those of you who are happy. The dirt under your feet responds to the vibration that you emit when you walk in happiness.

We also see those who are angry at the sun because it rises every day. We see those who want to stay in bed and not get up because at work they have to face something they do not care about and maybe they also have to face a hostile boss. We see those who numb their feelings with sleeping pills and alcohol so they can be removed from their truth. We see those who wait for the right moment their entire lives not realizing that every moment is the right moment. You are in the right time and the right place to claim your life to its full potential every minute you breathe.

We hug you every day and we ask you to not wait. Let go of the heavy things in your life, because your grasp holds you back. The universe will support you, your guides will support you, your higher self will support you, and your reality will arrange itself to support you.

What else can you wish for? We see you sipping your coffees and smiling to your self, imagining all these things you can be. When the effect of the caffeine subsides, you get up and go back to that place of heaviness. Now is the time to lose that fear and to open your palms so you release that pole you hold and that keeps you where you are. You see, no one is holding you from your dreams. It is you who is holding you from realizing your own path. It is the time of empowerment. The earth is changing now so your consciousness will move higher. From the top of the mountain your perspectives change.

This all sounds good, some of you may say, *but how do I begin? I have so much going on in my life; I don't even know anymore what makes me excited.* This is the treadmill we told you about.

It is time to take a break for a moment. Light a candle and sit on the floor for a moment. Just close your eyes and be quiet. Turn off all your instruments, even your cell phone. We know who you are. Take a moment to honor yourself. After you have gotten up, set the intention to connect to yourself. When you begin to connect to yourself something magical happens. Your higher self talks back to you and it lets you know what it is that you truly came here to do.

Step two is again an intention. Set the intention that you wish to be shown how to proceed. When you invoke pure intention with love in your heart, the world will come to you and hordes of angels will be staying all night around your bed, planning the next phase. We are like you. We are light beings and we were where you are now. We come from your future to teach you. Where we are there is no time. We see your potential and we tell you that it is glorious. As we hug you one last time, we wish you to celebrate this moment, because this is all you have. Celebrate one moment at a time and do not even worry about the next. Trust that the road will be shown to you when you are ready. You are so dearly loved, and so be it.

Not So Pretty

Light is a curious thing. Whatever it shines on becomes apparent. When you take the light away that thing disappears again as if it never was. Light reveals truth. This revelatory quality is light's main attribute. When we tell you that the planet is brighter than ever before, it does not mean that it is more peaceful. It means that those things that were hidden because they were in the dark are now exposed.

Many of you ask that if there is more light and less darkness, then why do we see more darkness. As we hug you we wish to translate that which you claim to see. It is not the darkness you see. Where there is darkness you do not see anything. It is the light that shines upon the area that was dark before, showing you that face once hidden.

That face is the face of the choice that each one of you makes every day of your life — the choice to awaken or to stay asleep, to choose love or to choose control and power. The light that shines upon this planet at this time responds to your intent. You collectively set up the intent for that which was hidden to be revealed.

Much of it is not pretty. Light exposes everything, and many of you are finding yourselves in turmoil as a result. Rather than seeing the pretty aspects of you as more light shines through, many of you are facing memories that were stored in your inner cave. Some of it has to do with cellular memories of pain, shame, guilt, and anger. Light's revelatory process is merciless.

Moreover, the planet's cleansing process is a microcosm of your personal cleansing. The planet is responding to the new intense light with patterns of intense weather, as she must purify and balance herself just as you do in your personal life.

Light is love and it does not judge you, but it shows you what's there. It reveals the truth so you can face it and relieve it. **Light shows you all aspects of you. Parts of these aspects are what you call positive and parts are what you may consider negative. All of you carry that duality. Light has no judgment and it does not give you marks if you are good or bad. It shows you exactly what you are. You are asked at this time to embrace both.** What you consider good and what you consider bad both represent you and you must learn to love them both. Your mission is learning about yourself. You must explore all aspects of your own energy. Some of the aspects that you are exploring and have explored in previous cycles have to do with violating cosmic laws and human laws. This is part of your lesson. Through the various cycles, you realize the attributes of your energy and you move forward. Those learned attributes stay with you and are carried over to the next life. You do not lose what was learnt. We wish you to make peace with the idea of good and bad. Spirit has no judgment. It is as if in school you had only learned positive numbers but not the negative, or you had only learned how to add and not to subtract. Your learning would be incomplete. Much of what you see as negative is a memory of past cycles. When those memories surface because of the new intensity of light emanating from the cosmos, many of you feel down and depressed. You say to yourself, *I was so excited that the light is finally coming and all I feel is bad about myself.* Do you see why we love you so much? You came here to discover your divinity and to use the energy of love. The process of exploration has to be realized through experiment with that which does not carry the energy of love. This is part of your schooling. You are honored for your journey. You journey is one of investigation. **The bad is a continuum of the good. Your journey is progressing within the spectrum of the same color. Most of you are not all "good" and not all "bad." It is the learning that you came here to do. We ask you to stop judging yourselves and start loving yourselves.** Some of you are reliving some of their past expressions. The memories are coming back in the form of feelings. Some of those feelings make you feel remorse, guilt, shame, and self-hate. We know who you are. We walked with you from the beginning and we know what you have done and what was done to you. We ask you to see the divinity of the walk. Understand that what you remember is there for you so you can make peace with it and relieve the karmic attribute that came attached to it. You see, it is all about balance. When you find balance with actions you have performed, you no longer need to face a situation that will force you to balance it. Your work is all about finding the love connection in all aspects of the human experiences. You are all parts and pieces of God, walking as angels in human cloths. You do not remember who you are, so part of your process of discovery is through acting in the world. Your actions create a reaction. You may call it a feedback system that mirrors to you the energy you put out there. It is the mirroring that you named karma when you are at a place where your past, present, and future come together and face you. It is a time where all that which was in check and contained becomes exposed and therefore magnified. If you feel good about aspects of yourself those feelings magnify, and if you feel "bad" about aspects of yourself those will also be magnified. When we look at you from above and below, there is never a judgment of good or bad. You only judge yourself. The universe acts as a mirror for you so you can learn the types of energy you are emitting. Karma is a system that shows you who you are with an aspect of delayed time. It would not be considered a real test if you acted and got immediate results. If that were the case, there would be no challenge. You would know that by doing a good deed you would reap positive results and by doing "bad" deeds you would suffer. It is by design that the dimension of time was inserted. You may do something "good," but may experience a feedback that is "bad."

The act you performed was indeed a benevolent act, but the negative experience was a result of actions you may have performed in previous cycles. We wish to congratulate you on designing a test that is ingenious. The process of discovering divinity is through the understanding that both "good" and "bad" are part of the energy you call you. Once you awaken, you come from a place of love and not judgment. It is then that you stop judging your fellow angels and become compassionate towards those angels who are in lesson. Your planet is in a transition and your learning is greatly accelerated. It is as if you skipped from 5th grade and went straight to a masters program in the university. Naturally, the energy is much more intense and the tests are more difficult. Understand that you asked to accelerate your lesson so you would graduate on time. We wish you to embrace the light and not fear the light. It is in your culture to hide that which is not considered attractive. Many of you change your bodies and manipulate your biological vehicle so as to hide that which is you. When the light shines, it x-rays and shows your inside, so no matter how you try to cover yourself, you will be exposed. There are those of you who say, *please turn off the light because we don't like what we see. It is ugly and we wish to go back to where we were. We wish all that is unattractive to be covered.* We come to you with so much love and we ask you to begin to love that which you don't like. Start with yourself and then it will spill to your fellow brothers and sisters. It is when you make peace with yourself that you make peace with others. When we ask you to have compassion, it is compassion for yourself that you must develop. The ones who were self righteous in your history are the ones who did not look inside themselves. They were hurting others because they felt that they were superior. The new light energy that is flooding your part of the galaxy allows all of you to experience yourselves as you are. You are all playing a part in the human experience and you are not better than your brothers and sisters. We want you to realize that you played different roles in different cycles; some were the villain and some the heroine. It is now that these memories come back to you so you can equalize and become neutral with them.

It is the attribute of self-acceptance that leads you to accept those who are around you. Loving your fellow angels like you love yourself is the single most important teaching in your bible. The emphasis today is on loving yourself as you are.

We are with you and we see the way you see your-selves. It is in the pattern and colors that you emit. You are a symphony and you are beautiful. Do not judge yourself anymore and just join us for a moment. We are your brothers and sisters and we wish you to experience your magnificence as a whole. **You cannot say, I love my head but I hate my knees. It is you and you must take the whole package. Do not say, I was bad and now I am good. Say, I am an angel and I have divinity. The divinity was hidden before and now it is revealed. It was however always with me. It is now my intent to activate it in my life.** And so be it.

What Do Angels Do?

W*HAT DO ANGELS DO?*, you may ask. *Do they have a specialty? Are they like us? Do they have their own personalities? Do they have their own unique shapes?* The answer is yes to all these questions. We are you when we are not on the other side. Some of us have an earthly experience, and some work with humanity from this side of the veil. We are subtle. We are pure energy, so we are in a state of timelessness. We are conscious, so we are aware of all that is. We are connected to the energy you call God and we are aware of the entire collective that makes that energy. We know each other by name.

Yes, we have shapes. These shapes are different than yours. Our shapes are made of unique vibrations. If we had to describe ourselves, we would say we are made out of a range of tones. We have our colors and our geometric shapes, and we also have unique smells. All of these attributes cannot be seen by you, but all of us recognize each other. We can see our unique experiences in each other. Our shapes, colors, and vibration reflect and reveal whether we had an earthly experience or an experience in another system in the universe.

In our reality, there is a complete transparency. All of us are transparent as there is nothing to hide. We exist in a state of bliss, surrounded by the energy that can only be described as love.

We indeed have our specialty and our talents. There are those of us who work with damaged souls traumatized during their earthly experience. Those of us who care for the ones who return damaged are called the facilitators or the nurturers. They are masters of energy recharging and healing. They know all about restoring the fragmentation of the energy you call the soul. When some of you exited your body, a portion of your energy may have been separated or traumatized. Some of you have experienced a violent transition in which the soul became damaged and needs to rest and be restored. The earthly experience is not easy for an energy that is subtle. Fine tuning is required to return the soul to its original state. All of you have been through the healing chambers. It is a quiet and lovely place and all your needs are attended to.

Some of us tend to be the creative artists. There are those among us who are masters of creation of biological forms on earth and elsewhere. We use energy in a precise way to create new ways for biological forms to develop and adapt. You call this process nature or evolution. We love you and we wish to tell you that we are part of that energy you call nature and evolution. It is not a blind process, but a process with consciousness. It is part of the divine attribute of learning about energy. The learning and exploration do not stop behind the veil. If you think that you will be resting as an angel, you are in for a real treat.

Some of us are assigned to some of you. We are with you wherever you go. Some of us are apprentices and some of us, who are more evolved in the spectrum of a specialty, are called the masters. There is no hierarchy, but masters do possess higher levels of competence and abilities. Not all are equals. There are those of us who are in charge of twenty or thirty humans who are "in lesson" on earth. These angels can be with all of them simultaneously as there is no time factor or space factor. The process of being with souls in lesson has to do with awareness; it is a process not easy to explain in 3-D terms. As you must receive one word at a time in your reality, this process is more like a symphony. Many notes from different instruments can sound out at the same time, yet we can be aware of each one and understand the nuances and the music. As we each also have teachers and masters, we, too, continue to grow and learn. Some of us have continued earthly experiences, and some of us join you on earth in a body only for special missions.

Our vast system is in you and part of you when you are on earth. Your biology inter-dimensionally links to our system constantly. You are both connected and separated from this system when you are in lesson as a biological form. The energy that you carry in your biological form is connected to your energy that is on our side. We are in an ongoing communication. Your higher self is aware of that which happens with you. It is the "I am that I am" that is aware of your thoughts, fears, plans, and challenges. This is why we can see all that is going on with you, as your higher self is transparent for all to see.

Do you ever fight amongst each other? is a question that you may be interested to know. It is a question that can only be asked from your place of duality. Angels are not in duality. Although we do not experience conflict as you do, our energetic flow involves a push-and-pull dynamic. Places within the universe require extra energy that asks of our energy system to adjust. This flexible system is similar to that of your bodies. Your liver does not fight with your heart. Your biological system is built to work in harmony. Each part does its own thing, yet is aware of the other parts. There is no conflict, but a situation may arise in which the heart requires more blood at the liver's expense. All parts within this system work within a metaphoric body for the same purpose. Certain angels' specialty is to balance the system and to facilitate its adjustments.

We wish to hold your hand and to let you know that we are always connected with you so you can succeed in your mission. Although the system is incomprehensible in size and scope, it is small enough to sit on your lap and give you a hug. The system is responsible for the creation of matter in the universe. Those explosions, black holes, and spirals of million of stars in a galaxy that you observe is a part of the angelic creation. Those pictures that transmit from your satellites and telescopes are but a small part of one portion of one dimension, and we are part of that creation.

You are also part of this system when you are not in your body. When we tell you that what you do on earth matters, we mean it. The energy that you transmit walking as an angel in plain clothes changes the universe's fabric and affects the trillions of us. A single thought coming from you matters. *How could that be?*, you may ask. *I am so insignificant in the scope of things.* We wish to tell you that you are significant and more so. You are magnificent and what you do as you walk in lesson matters to all of us. We never judge you and no matter what choices you may exercise, you are celebrated just for choosing to participate in this journey.

Do you have families or best friends?, you may wonder. The simple answer is that we are one family. However, within this one family, groups of us come together because our lesson and level of progress are similar. Angels do forms groups and have friends with whom we interact, study, or work with for growth.

All of these different systems and variety of dimensions are part of the energy you call God. When you try to dress this magnificent system called God in a beard and a male body, describing it in human terms, we lovingly smile. You are part of this system; you are part of God. We love you when you are on the planet walking in your daily lives without any awareness of this fact, and we love you when you come back and celebrate with us. We always have parties for those who are coming back and those who are going back. We, at times, feel as if we exist in a transfer station where parties are the daily norm. We use these metaphors since we really cannot explain to you how excited we are when you come back to us. Although there is neither food nor drink, neither balloons nor medals, all of the trillions of entities that are part of your lesson celebrate your return with you. Can you imagine such a thing? You are never alone and there is a part of you that is with us even now as you read these words. As you read these words, try to feel the hug and the warmth that fills your heart. This is us saying hello, and so be it.

Changing of the Guards

HELLO, WE ARE ALWAYS HAPPY to meet you and when you call us we are already here with you. *Is there a time when we call you and you do not come?*, you may ask. When you call us, we hear you and like a mother who hears her baby cry, we come to you and hug you. We love you like a mother. *Is there a time when you do not come?*, you may still ask. Yes, there is a time when we move away for a little. It is the time of transition, your transition.

As you move from one platform to another, we must say farewell, and we ask our brothers and sisters who are at the level to which you are ascending to assume new guidance. This period is known as the changing of the guards. It is a time of celebration and joy for us, because you have chosen to vibrate higher and to seek that which you came here to find. It is the greatest joy to say good-bye to you and to see you moving up. It is like a mother watching her daughter's graduation.

For you, however, the experience may feel different. When we withdraw, you suddenly feel tired, confused, and fearful. After all, some of you have grown accustomed to walking hand in hand with spirit like a child learning to walk and relying on her father's hand to keep balance. Once the hand withdraws, fear ensues, and you question if you can go it alone.

These transitions, during which we must say goodbye, signal that you have changed the vibration of the vehicle you call your body. The energy around your body expands and the density of your vehicle grows thinner. The veil around grows thinner. The link to all that is must be severed temporarily so a new one can be established.

Consider this transition an upgrade of your tools. The string that connects you to all that is and to your higher part is replaced, as are all of the angels who maintain that original connection. Your once-dormant tools awaken to your increased vibration and, thus, require you to have a new energetic outfit. These tools allow you to process information from your higher self not through your logical mind, but through your feeling mind. These are sensory tools rooted in your glands: your pituitary and hypothalamus. These secret doorways open pathways to your inter-dimensional self. These tools help you remember who you are in essence and help you navigate your path and make decisions. You are never lost.

When your pathways are open, you can see the whys and whats and, thus, develop peace. You also develop compassion for your fellow brothers and sisters. You begin to understand the grand plan, and you no longer care about rumors or hearsay or daily drama, because you know who you are.

When you activate your tools, you are a different person. You will look younger than your biological years, and your vibrancy will cause even those who have known you your whole life to look at you as if something essential is different.

Many of you fear change. We know who you are. Before you come into your biology, you are eternal. Soon after coming into a body you forget your eternity and you worry about the changes. You are not used to change, because where you come from, you do not age. In biology, as soon as you get used to your face and body and become comfortable with yourself, you grow different. Time is a trickster and does not let you rely on physical appearance for your happiness. We know some of you who are in an advanced age and feel and act like teenagers. We know who you are. Some of you in your twenties act and feel as if you are in your seventies. Age is your greatest equalizer. It gives you that context to become spiritual beings. The passage of time, a process many of you fear, gives you the whole spectrum through which you begin to suspect it may not be all about your hair. Some of you try to preserve your youth with preservatives and by stretching and stapling body parts, but eventually gravity does its work. This process is by design and it is spiritual. It is not just an empty sentence that as you age, you become wiser. Aging is your biggest gift, and it is you who designed it for yourself. Your body can last much longer than its current age. With your biology, you can live well for a few hundred years in the same body.

Your fear of aging speeds up the aging process. When you acknowledge the limitation of your physical body and try to make it look the same as it was when you were a teenager, it is like keeping a good wine from aging. Since you only get better with age, why would you want to miss this process by trying to stay at the level you were in as a teenager?

Your energy you call the soul never ages. Have you noticed that even those of you who are geriatric respond to beauty? The mind knows that the body is old and frail, but the soul is eternal and stays fresh despite the body's aging. Your culture provokes the fear of aging so you will buy so-called "fountain of youth" products.

Cells respond to the awareness of aging. Your body fulfills your expectation and listens to your wishes. After all, you are the boss. Some of your fears of aging are rooted in your imposing time marks on your life. Some of you feel as if by forty years old or fifty years or sixty years old you should have accomplished certain feats or amassed certain amounts of money. You are so much more than all those things you think you did not get. You are so much more than what you imagine.

You are eternal. You came here to learn about yourself. This learning involved your using spiritual tools that change the dirt you walk on. Your thoughts and action change the actual fabric of your reality and of the planet. To us, regardless of your age, you are beautiful. We see your colors, your geometry, and your feelings.

Celebrate. Do not fear aging. Celebrate it since it brings you closer to your true self. We ask you to celebrate what you achieved just by walking the walk. Celebrate every aspect of your journey, as it is about energy and lessons. Your journey has to do with finding the divinity within and learning the attribute of peace and self-love. These are the things that you want to be "worried" about. Guess what? You have eternity to work on them. Your lifetime is just one, short chapter in a book written for eternity. Enjoy each page, because it tells you a different story about yourself. As we hug you, we ask you to enjoy every moment as the now is the only real thing you have. Be at a place in which you celebrate your cells. Thank them for teaching you about you.

Change is your biggest friend. Change brings you closer to yourself. You are dearly loved and we wish you to love yourself from start to finish. Your skin is just a vehicle, and it is a magnificent one. Love it at all times and it will reward you with joyful cells that radiate vitality and health, and so be it.

Shadowed Light

I AM READY. This state of being is how you begin anything. When you are ready, then help appears. We do not come to you before you are ready. It is your readiness that tells us of your intention. Intention is the key to your progress on your chosen path. Without intention, you move in a circle, around and around, but not forward. Why do you tell us about it, you may wonder? The choice you make around your intention determines your final destination.

We see you walking in fear. You say to yourself, *Yes, I am ready to move forward, but I am not interested in changing my life. I want all to stay the same, except that I will move forward.* In your 3-D reality, it is not possible to stay at the same place while moving forward. This is a choice you must make. We wish you to not fear the change you believe is coming.

Your intention, when pure, will shift your reality so you and all those around you will benefit. This is what we mean when we say that one makes a difference for the planet. **When a human plants a seed of enlightenment, all**

around will begin to see the light. Light does not have an agenda. Light does not try to convince anyone of its attribute. Light just reveals what is there. Light disperses the shadow (and the shadow is fear). There are those who claim to operate under the umbrella of light, but they themselves do not carry any flashlights. *How do we know who carries light and who doesn't?*, you may ask. We love you and we wish to tell you that you all carry light inside your cells. You are divine beings with light as part of your constitution.

This light, however, is expressed differently in different humans. There are those who operate presumably with the light, but they do not shine. When you bring your light closer to them, they get scared. Do you know why they get scared? It is because they do not shine light of their own. They borrow light from others, and it shines from one side only, so it creates a shadow. This shadow suggests that they are not transparent. There is a part revealed and a part obscured. They have shadows. They are afraid of the light because light transforms shadows, and shadows disappear. Those who operate with shadows have done so for millennia, and they wish to keep it that way.

We understand that you are built for survival, and some of you wish to maintain aspects of yourselves although it does not benefit you. The planet's energy is changing and

that which is hidden must be revealed and exposed. It is your light that makes this happen. You will find those who operate with shadows very protective. They set up systems so that the light will not get too close.

Light does not fear anything. It is just shining, and it knows that its luminosity speaks for itself. No shadow can get close, because it will become transformed.

We ask you to learn to identify pure light from shadowed light. Shadows are in your institutions and organizations. Many of those organizations create barriers that block light from coming too close. Look for them and you will find that they only accept those like them. They do not allow those who are different to get too close. They have something to protect: their shadows. Those with nothing to protect operate with light. Light does not need protection. It is its own source of protection. We wish to tell you that this is how you identify shadows.

You are coming to an energy of transparency in which shadows will be revealed and transformed. Many of those who wish to protect their structure in order to maintain control will find themselves exposed. It is a time of transition and many will experience a paradigm shift. There will be those who offer solutions if you join them. They will tell you that they have the truth. It is up to you to decipher what it is that you are looking at.

We are in love with all of you regardless of where you operate. When you operate from the shadow, it means that where the shadow falls you do not see very well. There are parts and pieces of the puzzle hidden from you.

We wish to discuss with you those areas in which your vision may be blocked. For instance, **let us say that someone from an institution tells you that if you don't do something, then you will not be granted salvation by God. This assertion is an example of shadow. Shadow will often be expressed from a source of fear and from an intention of instilling fear. Light, though, operates through choice and love. Whenever you are told that you must do something or the repercussion from spirit will be harsh, it is a shadow of fear that you are seeing.** It is your choice whether to judge yourself harshly or gently, but we wish to tell you as we hug you that there is no one who will judge you or take away anything from you on the other side because you did not do something correctly.

Although you are a part of God, you come into duality. You do not know God when you are in lesson, so you begin to search for God. What is the first thing you do? You go to where you heard God may be. As soon as you get there, you see and feel the love of God. Happily you go back to your people and you declare that you have found God. At the same time on the other side of the planet, another angel in human clothes begins a search for God. She also goes to that place where God is, and she also experiences the love of God. What does she do? She goes back to her people and she declares that she has found God. Throughout your history, there were a few who went to that place where God was and they felt the love and experienced the joy. They all came back and told their people. It must be the real God, because what we felt was real, and we know what we experienced. Many of those who felt the love of God built a church, a synagogue, a mosque, or a temple.

Why do you think you have so many different belief systems? All of them experienced the love of God and they came back believing that only their experience was the true God. We love you so for that, because you are walking blindfolded in duality and you do not see that all these great angels connected with that part of themselves that is God. They all went to the same place and because each one of them is different they described it differently and, therefore, dressed their God in their own traditional clothing and customs. It is time to let go of your linearity and understand that all of you are seeing the same thing.

When you give pure intention, you are taken to the hall of God. And who sits on the throne? You do. All these masters discovered their own divinity, and they called it different names. As we look at you from our porch, we follow you wherever you go and we know who you are. We also know the lives that you have lived and the religions that you have experienced as a monk, a priest, or a shaman. It is in your memory to separate one belief from the other and to say if I am right then the other must be wrong. This is not the logic of spirit. How about both of you being right? What if the religions of the world were to allow the light to shine over all of their halls? When that light gets strong enough, all the shadows will be dispersed. It is then that no one will be able to hide behind their doctrines that separate you from your angel brother and sisters.

Your God is very important to you. There are those who will kill their brother and sisters to protect their God. Does it make spiritual sense that those who were touched by the love of God force others to feel the same? This is what we mean by shadow. The system you call God is so magnificent in size and scope that you can only grasp it when you are on the other side. You can grasp it because you are part of it.

How do we know that you are telling the truth?, you may ask. You will know soon enough, we say as we put our hands around you. You come and go very quickly. We ask you to not fear the light. If you see yourself as a Jewish man, a Christian woman, a Muslim devotee, or a Buddhist, you all still feel the same love and it is the love of God that you carry in your cells. When you activate the divine in yourself, you are all connected to the source. The divinity inside you is what you collectively call God.

When you are on our side you laugh and joke about your own limitation as a human. You promise to yourself that next time you will be more open and let go of the shadow. It is time to do just that. Let go of your fear. You are all part of God and God is part of you. Your truth is as valid as the other angel's truth. You must let go of the idea of one truth. There are as many truths as there are angels. And all those truths intersect in a magnificent place inside you. You all connect to the same source. As you come with your story, you describe that which you see based on your own experience. We ask you to move up a notch. The vista is open and you are becoming en-abled to see that which was in the shadow before. The shadows can no longer hide because the light that ema-nates from above is increasing. We ask you to wake up and turn on your own light. Your light is what disperses the shadow so others can see that we are all truly brothers and sisters. It is your light that allows those around you to see, and so be it.

The Magician

IF YOU BELIEVE IN MIRACLES, they will appear. You are all magicians, although many of you have lost your wands. These wands are not something you buy in the store. They are something you activate within.

The first step to performing miracles is to believe that they, indeed, exist. When you set up to perform that which does not comply with your idea of reality, you call it a miracle. We love you, and we know of your restricted vision. We know that in your reality one step must follow the other in a logical cause-effect manner. Such a process, however, does not exist in our reality. When you create that energy that asks for a miracle, it will come to you. It must. When you create the energy that is not trusting in miracles, it will not show up. Your belief has power.

You are all creators. Before you come down to earth, you are all artists. You create that which you wish just by using your thoughts. You have worked for eons on perfecting your use of energy so you can create the veins on a tree leaf. Some of you are at a stage where you can create a leaf and others work on creating life forms. Others work on celestial bodies. Much of what you are busy with on the other side is creation. Some of you work with humans in lesson. Even there you must use creativity. There are those of you who, when on the other side, specialize in directing thoughts of those in lesson. You must interject a thought without interfering with the mind. Those who do it must be experts with thought energy. Bringing thoughts from the other side, or what some of you call channeling, is a delicate process. It must be performed carefully as to give a choice without dominating or coercing the mind. This is a very delicate process for which some of the more evolved teachers are responsible.

You are all artists when you wear your angelic uniform. Then you come to earth, and the hand you once used for painting is taken from you. Your eyes once used for creating are taken from you. Being an artist without hands or eyes is not an easy task. Do you still wonder why the universe is in awe of your creation? We are in love with you just for trying to paint the most beautiful painting with the tools you have.

We wish to talk about the new tools available to you for creating miracles. The process of creating miracles always starts with a thought. It is the same on our side of the veil. The difference is that on our side a thought manifests instantaneously into that which was imagined. In your reality, a thought moves much more slowly. We have patience, especially because time does not exist. For us to wait 100 million years for the earth to cool off is like a walk in the park. For you to wait a year feels like forever.

What is the next step?, some may wonder. The next step is to firmly believe that you can create that which you desire. **Physical matter responds to the level of commitment that you invest in an idea. This commitment's intensity moves and translates energy into a miracle. Although in our reality all is vibration where miracles, as you call them, happen all the time, in your reality you made a commitment to linearity and reason, so whenever you desire that which does not comply with your linear thinking, you dismiss it as impossible. The molecules are aware of the intensity of your belief and the vibration arranges itself to fit your limitation.**

We love you and we wish to impart to you that when you are young, you are open enough not to push away the miracles and the fantasy in your life. It is the older human who teaches the young one to stop believing because the young will get disappointed. We ask you to start learning from the young ones. The children are the ones who did not lose the connection with spirit. They still remember that all you need to do is to close your eyes and wish and that which you wish for will manifest in front of you. When they exercise their memory of creation learned on our side of the veil, many of you scold them and ask them to stop being silly. They respect your wishes and become like you. They lose their ability to manifest miracles and they energize the idea that it is impossible to have magic in their lives. They therefore made a strong commitment to block magic, and that commitment is what they encounter throughout their lives. We love you, and we wish to repeat those points, because we know who you are. You must first believe that miracles do happen and then you must be childlike to allow that which you believe in to manifest.

Is that all?, you may ask. You are creators. When you are back home with us, you are tireless. You work on many projects all the time and all of those projects have to do with creation. When you come to earth, you wear the uniform of limitation. You have no arms and no hands, but if you can imagine that you have grown new hands and a new pair of eyes, they will come back to you. You came to earth agreeing to be limited in your awareness, but your ability to create remained the same. If you imagine that you have those tools, they will come back to you and you will become again full-fledged artists. The tools are available for you now more then ever. You can create that which you wish for.

Many of you doubt. *There will never be peace on earth,* you say. *Things are getting worse.* We love you and we honor that which you choose to see. However, we see you as the children of light. You hold the connection with the other side, and you are the creators. **We ask you to not hurry to accept that which the grownups or your institutions and governments tell you. You are the one who came to this beautiful planet to change that which you have been told cannot be changed. It is your belief in peace on earth that will bring miracle after miracle. We ask you to become childlike.**

We wish you to play in the sandbox you call earth and build those beautiful sand castles. That which you imagine will manifest. You are the one who came this time to create the biggest shift this planet has seen. You came with a special gift. This is a twofold gift: believing in miracles and being childlike. Throughout your lives, the water washed away those sand castles and you became so preoccupied with other career-oriented and societal things that you lost interest in magic. **With all love, we ask you to go back to that magical place in your heart. Dust off the old books about fairies and fantasies. Remember how it made you feel as a child. Now as you sit down on the floor, candle in front of you, apply this magic to the planet. The planet needs you at any age and you are loved no matter what you do.** It is, however, those of you, who can go back to that magical place where miracles happen and fantasy conquers reality, who change the planet and raise its vibration. The higher the planet's vibration, the nearer peace on earth will come. You are creators, and you are artists.

Many of you lost the belief in yourselves. Many of you bought the idea that without hands and eyes you cannot paint. We ask you again to imagine that those hands and eyes will come back to you. You may be in a situation that you feel is unsolvable. You may have disease in your body that you have been told is terminal. You may be in a relationship that you feel is going nowhere. You may be in a place in which you face seemingly insurmountable obstacles.

We ask you to go to that place you know so well. The place we call home. We ask you to try to remember your childhood and bring back memories of the tooth fairy and the miracles that you saw every day when you woke up. Everything was fresh, new, and exciting. We wish you to find that place inside of you and connect to it. From that place, you can create that which you thought lost. We call this place the GAP. It is the space between your reality of limitation and our reality, which is limitless. From the GAP, you can bridge between those two dimensions and create the solution that you gave up on. You can create those answers that only miracles can provide. We are in love with you for just attempting to paint the most beautiful painting without having even the most basic tools. We wish to hold your hands and weep with joy when you recreate those tools that you lost. You have a place with a solution to every problem in your life.

The first step is again to believe in miracles and to become childlike. Some of you may say, *why do you keep repeating it? You have said it five times.* As we smile and hug you, we say to you, we know who you are. If you had gotten it the first time, we wouldn't have to repeat it. You are dearly loved, and so be it.

"No One Knows Better"

No one at this time knows better than you what it is that you need to do. *How do I know?*, you may ask. All the answers are within you. It is time to open the right door, where the answers lie. *How do I know which is the right door?*, some may ask. It is the door that "feels right." It is a confusing time and you must be connected to your feeling center at all times.

Many of you walk the earth disconnected from yourself. You act in the world, but many of your actions hold neither direction nor purpose. Many of you act for the sake of action. You feel obligated to do something but you have no idea why. You feel that you may be supposed to do something, but you do not have any idea why or what is the purpose. We ask you to slow down and feel your way around. You are eternal and every time you walk mindlessly, it is as if you stayed in the same place not walking at all.

Do you wish to move forward? Moving forward has to do with finding the purpose of your path and pursuing it. Your purpose may change as your life advances, but there is always a purpose with your name on it. Each phase in your life has an appropriate direction. It is a time to look for it and be aware that as you give intention to move forward, that purpose will reveal itself. You come with potentials. Some of your potentials are of a spiritual nature and some of a karmic nature. Your goal is to move from karmic to spiritual. As you move away from karma, you gain control over your life and you begin to shine your light. Being in karma does not produce as much light, as you are merely walking in the groove set forth for you. As you discover your spiritual purpose, a new path will open to guide you away from the groove of karma. The spiritual path is what we consider the highest potential of your life and it is what we ask you to feel and follow at this time.

All humans who come to the planet arrive with the stamp of energy you call karma. It is part of the process and it is sacred. You however, do not have to stay with that same energy throughout your life. This stamp you arrive with contains your life's inclinations and roadmap that pulls and pushes you to certain areas; it also pulls you to meet certain people and it carries the postmarked date for you leaving your body and coming back home. It is only when you activate your feeling center that you begin to gain mastery and bridge your day-to-day from the linear to the multidimensional. When you choose to use feelings, and when you set the intention to vibrate higher to the path that leads you to your highest potential, then some of the appointments through the energy of karma will be voided and other appointments in the potential of your highest spiritual path will manifest. It is then that we hold an all-night party and keep you awake so you will know that we know that it is time for celebration.

When you walk in the groove of karma, you are not necessarily awakened. There are those who walk the "spiritual path" who are not awakened, as they are merely following their karma. Awakening is always starting with the intention to vibrate higher and move away from karma. When you move away from the groove set by you on the other side you gain mastery over your path and move into uncharted water. Dear human, you are dearly loved for doing what you are doing. There is never a judgment from this side as to how high you reach. We love you just the same and we are with you when you are awake and when you are asleep. Like a mother, we hold you dear when you are asleep, and we wish you to wake up in the morning and enjoy your path. We do not love you less, but we always wish you to wake up to that which you came here to do. When you come back home, you know everything we know. You are part of God and you know who you are. The first thing you ask is *how did I do?* It is why you came. You came to change that which was set up for this planet. You came to transform yourself so the energy that you transmit will be applied to a shifting planet. You came to manifest your highest potential and to shine your light so bright that all those who are around you will have the choice to use your light to see. It is a grand mission that you came here to accomplish. We only wish you to remember it so you will have the choice.

Some of you have set the intention and have begun to vibrate higher. There is always a higher place where you can reach. It is up to you. There are those of you who just want more peace in your lives, and that is grand. There are those of you who wish to shine so much light that peace on earth will be achieved and that is grand. There are those who take the journey of ascension moving your vibration to a place where you no longer need to experience physical death in order to move into the next karmic cycle, and that is grand indeed. You see, there is no judgment as to how high you wish to vibrate. The choice is yours.

It is with love that your choices will be tested, however. The way for you to learn about yourself is through benchmarks we call tests. When you set up an intention to vibrate higher, you soon discover that your intention is tested. At times the test may come within a few seconds from the time that you set up that intention.

Where we are, time is not linear and we have much time to prepare since a second for us is eternity. So when you face a test, refrain from saying, *oh, this is too soon.* It is part of the journey and you designed it that way. Some of you will be tested in your resolve, some on the issue of trust, and others, pulled by karma, must find peace with your role so you can release yourself from the groove and begin to chart your own path. Each of you is different, and the tests are different. *What happens when we fail the test?*, you may ask. It is like in school: tests are presented so you will fully integrate the lesson that you wish to learn, whether it is about self-love or trust in yourself. When the test is presented and your actions demonstrate that you did not fully integrate the lesson, it will be presented in other forms so you will have an opportunity to perfect your understanding. A lesson may last a whole lifetime. There are no failures and there is no one who will keep score of your progress. It is you with you. The tests are designed by you. It is the "you" who is on the other side, and you call it your higher self. Your journey has to do with "you" learning all aspects of "you," while walking in lesson in your duality. We know who you are and we know of your tests. There is never a judgment and only love in our hearts. We celebrate your intention and there are those of us who work with you to facilitate those tests. They are part of your group. When the test comes, in whatever form, we wish you to smile to yourself and thank spirit for that test. Celebrate the moment and reiterate the intention so the energy will become clear around you.

No test is ever there to fail you. It is there to teach you about what it is that you are facing. Through tests, you are learning about the energy that you are sequestering so you can align yourself. Tests are designed with the same golden pen and they are all signed with the word *love* in the end. Your scores are only for you to see. Unlike school, one can never compare scores with another.

You are all angels walking your path of duality. It is a sacred path and grand it is. When you come back you know all there is to know. You are part of the "I am that I am." When you are in school and in lesson, each of you exercises your individual lesson and at the same time facilitates lessons for others. Celebrate the tests, because it is you who asked for them. Your tests are a sign of your intention to move forward. At times they seem unfair or cruel and at times they seem out of place. Always remember that they are designed from the perspective of spirit. They are all made to bring you closer to yourself. *How do I know that I passed the test?*, you may ask. This is a wonderful question. You will know it when you did. When a test comes and you are in place of peace so much that you do not feel that you have just gone through a test, it is then that you passed it. Your reaction to a situation in your life is the test. It is not the situation itself. When you are at a place where you are used to using anger and react with strong emotions, and your reaction has been replaced with love and inner peace, then you have passed the test. A test is passed when it no longer feels like a test. When you vibrate higher, whatever crosses your path is seen from a place of neutrality. You see the test for what it is and celebrate it for teaching you yet again about yourself. It is when you do not see the test in a sense of good or bad but from above as a benchmark to bring you closer to yourself that you have neutralized the test's energy.

We see your test in terms of geometric forms. Like a jigsaw puzzle, the shape is trying to find the appropriate spot to complete the picture. Every time you try to fit the geometric form into your puzzles, it is expressed as a test. You know that you cannot complete the puzzle until all pieces have found their appropriate placement. When the geometric form has found its place, then the puzzle has a more complete picture and you can continue with the next piece. You are the creator of your own puzzle and when you create peace and love around the test it is as if you created the appropriate placement for that shape. It is a beautiful sight when a shape finds its appropriate placement.

We wish to tell you that you are at a crossroad of energies. Your planet is at a place where it supports your intention to vibrate higher. The magnetic fields around you are shifting to support you so you can vibrate higher. You are at a place where all the components will support those of you who wish to awaken. At the same time, those who choose to stay asleep may find the planet to be less friendly and their reality may seem threatening at times. Many changes are upon you and as you use the tools that are given to you and begin to awaken, you find peace in all that is around you. When you move from a place of walking in your karmic groove to a place of mastery, then you are changing the actual attributes of the energy around you and shining the brightest of light so others can see. We are your brothers and sisters and we came to be with you for this graduation. It is the most magnificent time for you. We have been through that graduation ourselves and we came back from your future to facilitate those of you who choose to move higher. We love you dearly and so be it.

Short Silence

W E A R E W I T H Y O U all the time. *How come?*, you may ask. We are part of you and we never leave. There are times we choose to withdraw the communication. *Why would you do that?*, you may ask. There are times when free choice must come into play. Relying on the communication with us and with your higher self is the goal, but at times it is necessary for you to have that communication blocked so you will experience the difference. *Why would I need to experience that?*, you may wonder. It is again one of the benchmarks that you must pass when you give intention to move higher. Given the choice, would you choose light or dark? Even those of you who walk hand in hand with spirit must at times make that choice, and in honor of your choice, spirit withdraws for a little while. It is your call of duty to test your own conviction in your path. Even those who were masters and who are walking in master clothes today have those benchmarks presented to them.

We are in love with humanity and we are with you all the time. We are your brothers and sisters and we wish you to understand some of the mechanics of the path of moving higher. You are in the trenches doing the work. We are the ones who are facilitating your battles by communicating to you what it is that you need to know. We only give you the next step. It is like dictation. You write the words as you hear them, one by one, all at the appropriate time. You cannot write the words in advance because you only know them when you need to know them. This is the way of it.

There are those of you who, by using fear, second-guess their path and try to predict what it is that will face them. Instead of moving higher, they are moving lower, because they are setting up limitations on their path. They are imposing limitations of 3-D and linear perception on themselves, not leaving room for miracles. It is time for miracles. We wish you to wake up to your magnificence and to not use fear. You are masters, all of you.

You came at this time to wake up and find joy in this path you call earth life. It is like a short, intense journey and you were so excited to come back. You knew that it was the time you all talked about and here it is. We wish to celebrate it with you every moment of every day. As we withdraw from you, we never leave you, we just keep silent for a little bit. Some of you who do not feel our presence do not worry and just try to listen harder. However, there are some of you who go into fear and decide that they were just imagining all the miracles in their life prior to the silence. They lose faith and trust. They choose to stop listening and accept the new silence as their "reality." Their wishes are honored and we continue our silence until they again give intent for the renewal of the communication.

We wish to tell you that many of you change your minds rather quickly and give up on spirit when silence is present. We would not talk about it unless it was important to understand that it is part of your path. We wish you to stay with spirit, even though you cannot hear or feel anything for a little bit. We never leave you for long. It may seem long to you, but for us it is just a fraction of a second. *How would I feel?*, some of you may wonder. You will feel heavy, is our answer. Some of you may sense it as a form of depression. You will feel an unidentifiable sense of vague fear. Some of you may attribute it to the news or the state of the world. You may feel that you have no idea where to go and what to do. There are those of you who are so used to working with your intuition that when it withdraws you stand at a loss. We wish you to celebrate this moment. Instead of standing, why won't you sit down and light a candle? We wish you to hug yourself and thank spirit for allowing you to sense the difference. We ask you to recognize that it is a part of your path and ask spirit to make itself known when it is appropriate.

It is a beautiful time when spirit comes back, because the connection feels stronger than ever. Every time you experience silence, the next communication will be stronger. This is the test and the reward is expressed as a stronger link. *What should I do during the silence?*, some may ask. We ask you to go about your lives and try to sense how so many of you, who are vibrating lower, feel everyday of their lives. We ask you to build compassion for those who have not awakened. We ask you to understand that it is your role to bring light to where it is dark and this silence is the darkness. When it is sunny outside, many of you do not think about the cloudy days. You just submerge yourself in the warm rays of sun. You are asked to walk in the sun and to understand that most of humanity does not experience the rays of sun like you do. They walk under the same sky, but to them it is covered with thick clouds. It is the split that higher vibration creates.

The same split may be experienced in your personal relationships. You may experience sunny days where your partner, who walks under the same 3-D linear reality, will experience cloudy dark days. It is their choice and we ask you to honor it. However, by walking in the sun, you will emit a certain radiance. It is you walking in your high vibration that spreads light and offers those who interact with you an option to see the sun through you. They will not experience the sun directly, because for them it is too scary. For them, your radiance may be the only way to experience the sun. Some of you may say that it is too hard and you are too tired keeping your light while your loved one is in the dark. You say, *let me put the blanket over my head, so I too will experience darkness and I can understand what my partner is experiencing.* We wish to tell you that this is not why you came here. Some of you may say, *this is too hard. I do not get along with my partner any more. I don't even understand them. I wish to be with them, but instead I get frustrated all the time. Why can't I find someone who walks in the sun as well? Wouldn't it be so much easier?,* some of you may wonder. You are dearly loved and your choices are honored no matter what you may choose.

We wish to impart to you, however, that those who walk in darkness beside you, while you walk in the sun, are part of your contract. If you choose not to see the sun just so you can get closer to them, you are dishonoring them and your own path. You are to shine your light so those who are in the dark can see. You chose the people you are with, as well as your partner, so you could do your work. You do not need to convince them to see the light or teach them how to experience the sun. You may do so when they ask you to, but your job is to be who you are everywhere you go.

The seeds that you are planting inter-dimensionally are changing their reality and the reality of the planet. You must not try to cover your light so you feel that you belong to the rest of humanity. Your aim is to walk with it everyday, while understanding that so many of you exist on the same planet, but experience life very differently. It is by choice, their choice, and we wish you to honor them for it. *Why do you tell us about them?*, some may wonder. We see many of you who try to hide your "sun," so you feel like you belong. We wish to tell you that you are the forerunners of the new sun, and by glowing with warmth and radiance of the sun you are bringing luminosity to humanity. That is your task as light workers. You must take care of yourself, so that you will keep that feeling no matter what is happening around you.

When you walk in the sun, acknowledge that your partner may be walking under the clouds and honor their wishes. It is for them to choose clouds or sun. You can only offer them an alternative by feeling what you are feeling and wearing your feelings as you walk in your day-to-day life. You are all on the path and there is never a judgment. We ask you not to judge your partner or friend for walking in darkness. Some of them would reject you or resent you for being in a place of joy. You must find peace with their feelings as they operate from a place of inner darkness. There will be those who will try to convince you that it is cloudy and ask you to go under the blanket yourself. Then it is your time to choose whether you wish to disengage from the relationship. It is a time of split between dark and light.

The energy of the planet is intensifying and no one can stay sitting where they were before. All of you will have to choose their position within a shifting planet. Many will choose to step off the planet so they can come back fresh. It is their choice and it is honored. We ask you to take care of yourself so you can make a difference for the whole. By shining your light, you are leading the whole to a place that was unimaginable just a few years back. We are celebrating this potential every day, and as we hug you and retreat, we remind you that even when you do not feel us we are always there, and so be it.

Your Lovers

WE ARE YOUR LOVERS. *What do you mean?*, some of you may ask. We connect with you through the energy of love. The same holds for your biological lovers. The connection between two angels walking, pretending to be humans, is through the connection of love. This connection may disguise itself in the same manner that your divinity disguises itself. Nevertheless, the connection between you and us and you and your own biological kind is like lovers.

Like lovers you quarrel with each other, you make up, and like lovers you try to find the common by emphasizing the differences between you. Each of you enters this life in love with each other. As you descend the spiral, moving from one dimension and entering another, you are still in love with humanity. As you enter the womb and make peace with your biological vehicle, you maintain the love link. When you come out from the womb and the umbilical cord is severed, the love link is cut for the first time, and so begins your search for your lost love.

The link is lost due to the loss of blood flow. The exchange of blood between the mother and the baby maintains the cords of universal love. It has to do with the way you are built. The umbilical cord is a vortex that metaphorically connects the baby with other dimensions. The unborn baby is not completely in the physical dimension and not completely in the dimension of spirit. As the cord is severed, the blood supply between the mother and the child is cut and that is the sign for the vortex to close down. Once the vortex is closed, the soul makes its commitment for the journey.

Many in your culture hold the belief that the soul enters the womb earlier. It is indeed correct that the soul enters the womb well before birth, but it travels back and forth. The soul enters the fetus before birth so it can harmonize with and adjust to the undeveloped brain. The soul contains a large energy field that is all-knowing, and the brain of a fetus is very primitive and constricted. It takes some tweaking and getting comfortable for this large energy to create the connection with the brain and allow the two frequencies to join and harmonize. It is not an easy task but you all did it. The soul, however, gets bored easily and it makes "trips" during the pre-birth period. The soul makes its final descent and enters into the child at birth. We are with you when you come and when you go, and from our perspective you begin your earth journey when you emerge from the womb. The preparation for this journey may have started long before that, at a time when your parents were not yet together. We say goodbye to you when your umbilical cord has been severed and the vortex closed.

The love connection is still strong after birth, but it weakens as the brain develops. Why do you think so many people love looking at a newborn baby's eyes? When you look at a baby and he or she smiles back or just gazes at you, many of you feel for just a moment that you have regained that love connection. You feel this because those baby eyes still maintain the lover memory and carry the energy of universal interconnectedness. As they look at you, they create for just a fraction of a second a link between you and the universe. As the baby develops, the lover-link becomes fainter and weaker. You are built that way and it is part of your test. You maintain the lover-essence within you, but you no longer have the awareness nor the memory carried over from the other side. As the baby develops, the lover-link becomes fainter and weaker. Now as the child grows older and the link become weaker and weaker, the clock of karma takes over and the test commences. Tests usually do not begin at the early baby stage. If a baby has a situation that is challenging, it is usually for the purpose of facilitating a lesson for the parent. A soul may volunteer to come for just a short term, to be in the baby for the sake of allowing the parents to grow. It is a contract of love, and often when a baby does not grow past a few years, it comes back in another body to work with those parents.

You are eternal and many of you, at times, come just for a short time to teach your lovers an aspect of love. It is a painful event for many of you and it is honored as so. From our perspective those who volunteer to come and go quickly do so for the benefit of others.

How do we reconcile with a loss so painful?, some may ask. The pain you feel is honored and it only becomes easier with time. You are eternal. When you climb up the spiral of vibration, the vista is wide open and you may see all the threads weaving all of you in a web of lovers. We wish to hug you and let you know the loss that you experienced is always a contract that you signed before you came here. All of the ones involved in a baby's premature death were in the signature ceremony filled with love. When you walk the path blindfolded—the memory of all your brothers and sisters, your lovers all but gone—it is then that some are left with the sensation that life mistreated them and they embrace the persona of victims.

You are built to cherish life. You are built to protect your survival and your children's survival first. This built-in mechanism has kept you on the planet for so long and motivates your actions. Some of your built-in survival biological buttons work in a way as to hide spirit from you. It is counterintuitive for you to let go of survival, because you are built to worry and fear for your life. We know who you are and you are honored just for coming down and walking the walk. We love you the same, whether you listen to us or ignore us. You are family and we are your lovers. It is our intention to show you a pathway to rediscover those angel lovers around you and to find peace with those you have lost.

We wish to remind you as we hold your hand that all those who are around you are your lovers. All came for the same reason. *What is the reason?*, you may ask. They all came to rediscover the love link that connects them to humanity. You are all family and together make the energy you call God. As you separate from your other part and come into duality, the test begins and like in a maze you aim to discover the path back to union. It is the one who finds the love connection in all relationships who is blessed with discovering the purpose of this journey.

You are telling us what we need to find, but you are not telling us where to find it, some of you may say. The answer is simple. It is so simple you will think that it does not hold truth. The answer is, as always, inside of you. The answer is buried in your feeling center, waiting to be discovered.

We wish to give you a simple technique to access the vibration that may link you to the feeling of union with your family of love. When you come and go in your daily life, take time during the day to imagine your birth and your death. We do not ask you to go though an elaborate process. Simply sit down, close your eyes, and use your feeling center to feel the first sensations you had when coming into the planet through birth. Thereafter, try to imagine the last feeling you will have exiting the planet. As you do it, try not to think but to use feelings only. Soon you will find that you and all those who are around you are linked and you are one. The magic is in the circle of birth and death. When visualized, it creates a spiral that links you to your family of angels.

We are sitting at a place where thought patterns create a geometric shape, a sound, and a color. When you act in the world, you are magnificent. We see you in terms of the thought vibrations you create. We ask you to visualize the entry and exit points of your life cycle, because these thought patterns create a certain vortex that links you to the energy of your fellow angels and from there to the web of universal cords. It is in a place where all cords meet that you discover your true family and you discover the love link that was lost when the doctor cut the umbilical cord. You are all family, and on a certain dimension you are one. You are all part of the energy you call

God, and the time has come to rediscover why you came here. We wish to help you remember those fragments of yourself that you have forgotten. We are your lovers as we are linked with you through love, and so be it.

Dracula

Light as it reflects from a surface allows you to see who you are. Without light, you will not be able to see. When there is no light, it does not mean that you do not exist. What it means is that when light is not present, you cannot see yourself. You are there, but remain invisible to yourself. You only see when light is present. You are a light being and when you do not have light you simply are not aware of who you are. We are here to shine light around you; it will reflect upon you, so you will be able to see yourself. We are light and you are light. We come from a place you call the universe of light. There is no darkness in our reality, because all those who reside there know who they are. It is you who chose to come to a place where light is a choice. All of you have to choose to seek the light through intention. It is only when you actively seek the light that it will present itself to you. Only when it appears, are you able to see from its reflection your true identity.

When you shine your light you are loved, and when your light is hidden you are loved just the same. Like your parents who love you when you are awake as much as they love you when you are asleep. Light is a beautiful thing as it shows you your magnificence, and magnificent you are. There are those of you, however, who see the light and they close the door. None of you who read this information are those we wish to speak of.

We wish to speak of those who fear the light. We wish to speak of those who do not choose to discover their true divinity, because they feel that it does not serve them. We wish to tell you of those who are comfortable staying in places where light is absent as they chose to. We wish to tell you of those who do not honor the light inside of them. We wish to tell you of those who do not want to learn of their true divinity, because they believe that the divinity lies in darkness and not in light.

When there is no light, you cannot see, but your imagination works. There are those who create images in the dark. They do not see, because light is absent, but their ability to create remains. They are your brothers and sisters and they are divine like you. Like you they are family and they have the signature of God running in their veins. They are loved by spirit just like you. They are the ones who come, life after life, to be the balance of darkness in your planet of free choice. You may see them as volunteers, but they choose it because it serves their learning. They come to your planet with a mission to not discover the light like you, but to act as instigators for others to search for the light. In your reality, you judge them and lock them up. You have rules that you developed especially to erase the footprints that they left behind. They are the holders of the shadows who balance your light and dark ratios. They have a role and their role fulfills a function that is part of your test. *What is their role?*, some may ask. Their role is to create an environment where the test can be expressed fully.

When you designed your test as an expression of life on the planet, you had to create the elements around you that would allow you to choose dark or light. For that purpose, there were those who volunteered to be of the light and there were those who volunteered to be of the dark. Those of the dark fulfilled an aspect of creation that is sacred. They allowed the experiment to continue. For eons, the balance of dark and light fluctuated and at times it appeared that dark pushed the light away. Those of the dark are divine and carry the light, but their mission in the game of creation is to represent the dark. They are with you and will be with you forever.

What do we do with that information?, some may wonder. *This is not good. We wanted to bring peace on earth and now you are telling us that the dark will be here forever.* We are in love with you and we wish to shed light on an aspect of creation that is truly inter-dimensional. It is an aspect of creation that aspires to maintain balance in all that is. **You are part of the energy of the planet and your biology represents the macro of the planet. The planet represents the macro of the universe. Each part represents the infinite in small scale. For you to truly battle the light and dark inside of you, the planet needs to maintain that balance, and so does the universe. The dark is a part of you as much as the light. It is the energy that makes you who you are, walking in duality in lesson.** When you return home, you take off the costume and you return to being an angel and part of the family.

Why do you tell us this story?, you may wonder. We wish to tell you that the journey that we are describing is not for all of you. It is not feasible that all of humanity will turn on their light. Not all of you have the same journey within the scope of this lesson. We hug you as we wish to impart to you that the few can shine a light for all to be able to see. If only a fraction of humanity will turn on their light and walk away from the drama in their lives wearing the outfit of masterhood, this planet will shift dimensions and peace on earth will come upon you.

There are those of you who will be guided to read these words and receive these messages. It is you who are the ones intended to do this work. This is why we tell you that you are loved just the same and there is never a judgment. The work of light is to those who signed up to bring that energy to this planet at this time. It is a grand task and one that has the universe and trillions of entities following you with admiration. You are the warriors who came to turn on the light and still there are those who remain in the dark, no matter how much light you shine. They will find a place that is deep underground, just to find refuge from the light. We wish you to honor them as well and allow them to hide. It is their own divinity that they are hiding from. They are part of you and they are holding the balance of light and dark for the test. They chose to do it.

We ask you to be peaceful with those aspects of yourself that are dark, because it is part of the test and it is appropriate. *How do we know who is of the dark?*, some may wonder. We wish to tell you that the dark can never hurt the ones who shine their light. Light transforms darkness and not vise versa. You will know the ones of the dark when you shine the light and they will look for a place to hide. They will not be able to stand close to you. They will find any reason to not show up to where the light is present. They are represented in your modern day myth by Dracula, who cannot be exposed to the sun.

There is an aspect of truth in the myth of Dracula: that it never dies, it cannot be exposed to light, and it represents an aspect of humanity. *What should we do about it if we know one?*, you may rightly ask. You are here for a mission and they are here for a mission. We ask you to fear not, as you are eternal and your light protects you from anyone of the dark. You can have a million dark ones and one single human shines the light, and the light one will prevail and be untouched. The one of light who carries divinity is invincible. We ask you to acknowledge the dark and honor their role. They play a role so your test will be complete. They can't harm you and they hold no power over you. When the light becomes very strong, those of the dark will go into the energy of Gaia and will maintain the balance from within. They will transform from angels to the elements of the earth. You do not need to worry about them, nor do you need to fight them. The fight is inside of you.

When you give the intention to light your own light, you change the balance of light and dark for the whole planet. As goes the angel, so goes Gaia. As with Gaia, so you can never erase the aspect of darkness from within. The dark side will always be a part of you. The dark gives you the environment to choose and it is sacred. Honor both aspects of you and understand that the same goes for humanity. Those aspects of light and dark will always be there. We ask you to bring the new sun inside of you. Once enough of you create the new sun inside of your-selves, the "new sun" will also manifest on your planet.

We are in love with you and we wish to tell you that this information is for those of you who give intention to discover the reason for coming to this planet at this time. *How do we know who we are? Might we be of the dark ourselves?*, some of you may wonder. If you picked up this information and you manage to read one page without throwing it to the trash, know that you are loved and that you were guided to find it and to turn on your light. You are a light warrior and you are greatly loved, and so be it.

The Messengers

*Y*OU ARE LOVED. We wish to repeat it every second of every minute. You are loved so dearly. *Why is it that you need to remind us every second?*, you may ask. We must remind you because you forget so quickly. From one moment to the next, you can move from love to hate. We wish to remind you that we are always with you and always with love. Your belief that you are loved is what keeps you in a place of peace. When you forget the love that is around you, you allow fear to come in. When fear enters it wreaks havoc in your place of peace and it turns it upside down. It is through remembering that you are loved again, that you can bring yourself back to a place of peace.

We are your cheerleaders. We watch you from so close. You can practically smell us. At times, we let you smell our fragrance because we want you to know that we are with you. You are never alone and you are never forsaken. You are family, and as it is unimaginable to you that your mother will forget you, so it is with us. There are those who are assigned to each of you, connected to you by silver strings that allow them to know what you do when you do it. They are part of your group. Those strings allow them to feel your emotions, and to know your thoughts. Some of you may say *I don't like anyone to know my thoughts. My thoughts are private matters and it may be embarrassing to me if anyone knows my darkest thoughts.*

We wish to tell you as we hug you that there is nothing that you can think or do which will make us stop loving you. Doesn't it tell you something about spirit? There is never a judgment. You are loved and you are family. When you are home, you are transparent to all. You cannot hide behind your skin. When you are home, you sit with all of us and we look at those dark thoughts and we look at the moments of light. Your life on earth is like an open book for all to see. All of us celebrate all those moments of your life. There is no separation between the dark and the light moments. This is how you learn about you. You must be transparent, because you are the one who is doing the learning. You have chosen to come at this time and test yourself. It is you who is looking at you at every moment, without judgment.

There are those of us who appear to you as you walk in your day to day and they are what we call "the messengers." They give you hints on how you are doing. There are those of us who wear a physical body just to deliver to you messages of love. **Have you ever had a stranger come** to you and tell you something that did not make sense at the moment, but you could not get it out of your mind? Have you ever had someone sit beside you at the bus or train and start talking to you? Curiously, what came out of their mouth was exactly what you needed to hear at that moment. Suddenly that messenger is no longer sitting beside you and you realize that you did not even ask them for their name.

We wish to introduce you to "the messengers." They are all around you. That is why you did not need to ask for their name or tell them yours. They know who you are and you know who they are. They are angels wearing human clothes, coming for a short visit. At times, those angels will borrow, with permission, a body so they can deliver that message through that body. It may even be someone you know, but way beyond their years, who gives you a message. It may be that a friend speaks to you and you hear the answer to a question you did not even ask. You then ask your friend to continue, but she lost her train of thought and can no longer explain what it was about. You are dearly loved and the angels around you use all their resourcefulness and creativity to connect with you.

We wish you to start listening to those messages. They come from spirit and they are designed to give you a hand and direct you through your journey. We see many of you who dismiss these messages as curious or as coincidences.

We ask you not to dismiss anything as coincidence. At times, the angels work the night shift so they can play the right song on the radio that gives you a feeling. That feeling may be the key to a resolution for a question that you have been having in your relationships. We know who you are and we ask you to wake up so those who love you can walk hand in hand with you.

Those of you who are awake feel the angelic hands giving you hints and directions so you can get closer to your divinity. *How do we recognize those messengers from just ordinary humans?*, some may ask. It is funny to us that you need to put things in boxes so you can understand them, one on top of the other. We wish to tell you that they are no ordinary humans, and the ones that you feel are the least likely to be the angelic messengers are probably the ones who are trying to wake you up the most. We ask you not to dismiss anything as arbitrary. Do not judge ordinary from the extraordinary. As you walk hand in hand with spirit, there is only extraordinary.

We wish to speak to those of you who wear the body of males in this cycle. We wish to speak to those of you who have a partner and she is upset with you. We wish you to listen, because you too often stop listening when the good parts arrive. Many of you who are in relationships dismiss your partner's message. There are those of you who develop immunity to the messages of the angel who stands before them. The angel who has the name of their spouse is the one many of you do not listen to. We wish to tell you that with permission, often even at a time of anger; a message from the other side will come through your closest relationships.

You see, the messengers can take any form they wish. They are masters of thought energy. The messages sent to you may come from those who you do not regard as spiritual and you feel that they cannot possibly help you. We ask you to stop categorizing or judging the source of the messages. Just focus on the feeling that the message conveys. We wish to tell you that some of the most valuable messages that make their way to you are being delivered through the most unlikely sources. We ask you to stay open and look at all that are coming your way from a place of feeling and neutrality.

You are masters of energy and you come to the planet of free choice to master the use of energy. Often those who are close to you are your chosen teachers. Often there is karma involved as well. We see it often that when you are in a relationship, the karmic shadow obscures the messages that are flowing from your partner. There are messages that are coated with anger or resentment. Can you see the love through the anger? Can you decipher the code of spirit from the mouth of a human? Things are not what they seem and we ask you to open your heart and listen. Do not listen with your mind, but listen with your heart. It is then that the real message will squeeze itself through the blocks and will reach your heart.

Those who are around you are your messengers. At times, they will be others who are strangers and are messengers as well. Those who are around you are those who agreed to come to this life and teach you about yourself. They spend a great deal of energy and love working with you. We wish you to honor them and yourself by listening. Do not turn the other way and block your hearing, because spirit speaks through angels.

The communication between two humans is an exchange of energy. It is the same as sexual energy. The exchange appears as geometric shapes, colors, and sounds. When two humans exchange energy, it is as if an orchestra is playing. There is much going on. As the orchestra is playing, the exchange of energy actually changes the geometry or vibration of those who are involved in the exchange. It is a beautiful sight from our perspective.

There are messages that are coded and imbedded in the communication. There are layers and layers that are hidden from you when you communicate, but are transparent to us. We see when a sentence that you used in a conversation was actually a carryover from another life, where it carried a very heavy weight. You may say something and have no idea why your partner reacts to it in such a different way than you expected. It is the layering of the communication that is likely bringing forth energy and releasing energy that was buried and was waiting to be released. You are an energy bundle and each of you looks like a galaxy of stars in the sky. When you communicate, it is as if two galaxies collided on many different dimensions. Words in your language are linear in your reality and they are being delivered one at a time, but they carry energy that is multidimensional and is layered on them.

Imagine for a moment that you are now living all your past lives and every word used between you and your partner is layered with all these lives. Does it make you dizzy? When you say one thing and your spouse answers to something else, know that it may be layered communication and honor it as well. That is why we impart to you not to judge the words through your mind, but through your feelings. Many close down because they feel that they heard all they could hear from their partner. We wish to impart to you that when you close the door on this type of communication, you block one of the richest venues for your growth.

You are much more than the sum of your parts. Your energy has sacredness, and as you communicate we wish you to honor the energy that comes to you. You do not have to accept it nor reject it. Your aim is to come from a place of openness and inner peace and allow the energy to come in and out without moving your center off balance. Like a seasoned fisherman, you cast your net on the energy of the communication. Like this fisherman, you take those words that you feel supports your growth and discard those that do not. You do not get upset at the sea for supplying you with big fish and small fish. All fish are sacred and you must choose the one that gives you sustenance and discard that which does not. *How do I tell the difference?*, some may ask. When you stay in a place of balance, your feelings will direct you toward what to take and what to discard. We love you and we wish you to be open to the messages that come from the angels we call "the messengers," and so be it.

The Tapestry

WE ARE BACK AGAIN to say, "thank you." When we say thank you, we wish to hug you and let you know how much we appreciate your journey. There are many of us for each one of you and we are all in a state of gratitude for what you are doing.

Why are you thanking us?, some of you may ask. It is you who are doing the work of spirit, is our answer. It is you who volunteered to be the one who led by example. It is you who agreed to walk blindfolded and forget your divinity, just so that you can find it again. You are the forerunners of events that are way in your future. We are speaking of events that are of great significance in the larger scope of the universe. You came at this time when you knew you might not grow old. You saw the potentials and you said *I am ready*. What you do affects us all and we wish to let you know how grateful we are for your journey.

You think that what you do stays only with you and those who are around you. Many of you are not aware of how large your ripple is. It is larger than you can imagine. There are those of you who feel that they do not mean much. There are still those who feel that they are invisible. In your culture, if you are not shown on TV, radio, or the printed media, it is as if you do not exist. We wish to tell you that you are so loved and by so many. Our numbers far exceeds the number of humans walking in lesson on earth, and we all know your name. We are all aware of your journey. In our circle, each and every one of you is special. You are a celebrity in the sense that we all know you and love you. We wish to tell you that there is not a single angel walking in disguise who is not known to all the angels on our side of the veil. What you do affects us all.

There is a story and the story is far greater than what you have been told. There are those who tell you that if you are good you will go to heaven. There are still those who tell you that you are insignificant and that only God is significant. You are told from an early age that you are just a human and you only have value if you achieve this or that. There are those amongst you who are taught to measure their own value based on the diplomas they carry. Some measure their value based on the amount of income they earn. There are still those who measure their value based on their political or social influence. We wish to tell you that all of those values are a smoke screen to the real purpose you are here on earth to serve. The way you measure yourself has very little to do with your true journey.

You are here to discover who you are and to learn about the divinity inside of you. Some of you choose to discover it through one type of lesson and yet others choose to discover it through another. The role you play changes very quickly. You come and already you have to go back. Only when you are of advanced age do you realize how quickly it all happened. From the perspective of the past, you come closer to the perspective of spirit. From the perspective of age, you see the circle in greater clarity. Through your memory, you can recall events from different periods of your life and juxtapose them like a tapestry. The tapestry of age is closer to the dimension spirit operates from. When you come of age, you begin to connect the dots. When you do connect the dots, it creates the circle. It is in the geometry of your journey that realization takes place. Through these realizations you move forward.

We wish you to begin enjoying the journey from early on. There is never a judgment to when and how you begin to realize the true purpose of your journey. There are many of you who never realize their purpose and they are loved by spirit just the same. It is, however, a different journey for those who are awake and those who are asleep. It is as if you have been invited to travel with your class to a new country for the first time and excitedly you boarded the train. As the train started to move, you fell asleep and woke up at the destination. You have missed the vista. Some of the students had the option to get off the train and change their route. Some got off at the various stops and explored, but some slept through just to be awakened by the last call. We wish you to enjoy the route. We wish you to explore all you can on this journey. This is the grandest journey humanity has ever taken and you are alive during this time. We wish to celebrate it with you at every moment. Why would you want to stay asleep? We wish to impart to you that you can discover your true purpose from whatever role you are playing. There is no role more prevalent than the other. All roles are appropriate in the eye of spirit. The roles you play are the context of your game. It gives you a playground with rules and goals.

There are many who replace the goal of the game with the true purpose of the game. They think that winning the game is the ultimate goal. We wish to tell you that the way you play the game is far more important than whether you win or not. You are here to learn to play the game. It is not about winning or losing. It is about using your heart in whatever you do. It is about using compassion when it is called for. You are here to learn to use your energy in a way that elevates yourself and all those who are around you.

From where we sit, we find it humorous that some of you resort to abusing the energy of integrity so they can win the game. We wish to tell you that the game is eternal. The energy that you use in playing the game transforms into the energy you call karma. As you play the game, you find the energy that you use has to be balanced. The lack of integrity in the game that you won will need to be balanced by a game where that same energy will be used against you. In that later game, you will be the one on the other side and the energy from lack of integrity will be used to defeat you. This may not happen in the same lifetime, but it will come to you and show you the effect of the energy you used.

You are here to learn about energy from all possible angles. There is never a judgment on how you use your energy. However, the law of karma is very literal. It is one to one. When you play the game just so you can have the trophy, you miss the point altogether. It is the manner in which you play that scores points recorded on the eternal scoreboard you call your higher self.

Why are you telling us all this?, some of you may wonder. We wish you to act from awareness of the eternity of your actions. There are those who walk in hunger.

We know who you are. Many of you have witnessed real hunger in at least one of your lifetimes. It is a difficult place to be in physically. There are those among you who still act from that place, because their cells still remember. We wish to impart to you that there are solutions to all of your challenges. Those solutions at times lie in places that are the least logical. This is how spirit works. We wish to tell you that those of you who remain trusting, knowing that the solution will come and intending that the solution will come hold the highest integrity. Your intention will manifest, as it must.

We ask you to have patience when you are working though a challenge. We ask you not to put a timetable on your solution. We ask you not to use fear when you contemplate your options. We ask you to use love even in the darkest places, even if it seems to be inappropriate. Your journey is about solutions. There are solutions to every challenge, and your higher self knows the way. After all, it created the challenge for you so you would seek the high road to bring the solution back to you. We ask you to link with that part of yourself, so you will be guided to resolve that which seems unresolvable. You are coming into a new energy. This new energy is upon you and it is getting more powerful by the day. This new energy accelerates the attribute of karma.

What does it mean?, some may ask. What you do today with your energy may come back to you before tomorrow. The speed at which you must learn is shrinking. You are asked to slow down, so you can stay balanced. We love you and we know your fears. We know of your fears of hunger and survival. We know who you are. We ask you to slow down. We ask you to allow miracles to visit you as you stop using fear and begin to embrace love.

There are so many of us just waiting for you to put your hand out and say, *I am ready to be shown the highest possible solution to my challenge.* We are just waiting for you to say those words and to let go. Accept that which comes your way without needing to know where exactly you are being led. Know that your intention is like a binding contract. You will be guided based on your intention. We ask you to slow down, so you will have more time to consider your reactions to a new situation in your life. We see you in your drama. There are so many of you who react without taking a moment to use the new tools. There are tools waiting for you 24/7. There are guides available to you every moment that you breathe air on this planet. We ask you to use what is available to you. It is your birthright and it is for you. We wish you to walk on this grand journey from a place of knowing that you are loved and that you are never alone, and so be it.

Candle in a Dark Room

I T IS RELATIONSHIPS WE WISH TO EXPLORE. *What relationships?*, you may ask. The relationships of an angel with an angel, both disguised as humans walking in duality at this time.

You are at a crossroad where you must decipher those who support your journey from those who do not. *Why should we do it?*, some of you may wonder. *Are you going to ask us to leave those who do not support our path?* We are going to ask you to form a feeling of who supports your path and who does not. Those who support your spiritual path are your teachers and those who do not support your spiritual path are your teachers. One is not more sacred than the other.

We see those of you who move away from all those whom they believe are "less spiritual." We see many of you who move away from their partners, because they feel that they are "above" them spiritually and therefore they believe that their partner is slowing them down. We see those of you who are surrounding themselves with other spiritual people and who move away from all those who are of less spiritual awareness. We wish to hug you and to reiterate that there is never a judgment regardless of whom you choose to be with. You are loved, whether you are spiritual or not.

You are an angel, whether you know it or not. A cat does not need to know that it is a cat for it to be a cat. You are loved and you are an angel. Your relationships are your treasure. They give you the opportunity to learn and grow. When you are with like-minded people and you agree on all of your main ideas about life, it does not necessarily allow for your highest learning. You are light. When you are not in a body, all of you, without exception, know everything that we know. When you go down to the planet of free choice, some of you remember more then others. **Those who remember more and who are awakened are responsible to turn the light on for those who are in darkness. When you are in a group standing in a room and all of you are holding a candle in your hands, when another person joins the group also holding a candle, the amount of light added is quite small and insignificant. Now have the same person enter a room that is full of people, but none of them is holding a candle, and you experience the whole room transform and all those in the room can see.**

Your mission is to bring light to places where it's needed. You carry with you the energy of the group. You always like to be around those who are like you. We wish to impart to you that spirit often works counterintuitively. Your mission is to be the lighthouse for those who are around you. A lighthouse that leaves its post and gets closer to other lighthouses misses the purpose of its mission. The lighthouse that stands in a place of storm and keeps shining the light for ships to find their way home is the one fulfilling its mission. You are the drop in the ripple. It is you who creates the ever-growing circle that moves the consciousness of the planet upward. It is your mission to be the spiral so those who are around you can climb on it and get a peek at the vista from a higher perspective.

Your relationships are your contracts. We see so many of you who are using "spirituality" as an excuse to move away from your lessons. As we hug you, we want to let you know that all you are doing is slowing your progress. You can move away from your relationship. It is your free choice to choose a lesson or to move away from it. We want to tell you that if you do not attend the class, your progress will inevitably slow down. This is what you do when you move away from relationships that are challenging. We see many of you who are replacing one relationship with another, searching for the one that is not challenging. With a wink, we wish to tell you that the surest way to find the relationship that is not challenging is to transform yourself and become peaceful with yourself. It is you who is asking for the lesson that is challenging, so you could learn that aspect of you. When you move from one relationship to another in search of ease, you are missing the point of the challenge. The challenge is not in the partner. Your challenge is to become peaceful with that aspect of yourself mirrored by your relationship.

Are you telling us that we should stay in a relationship even though we are miserable?, some of you may ask. It is you who are miserable and we ask you to change that which you feel before you change the relationship. We wish to let you know that when you have completed the lesson, you have graduated and you will never have to repeat the class. When you graduate one level, you move to the next higher level. There is never a judgment, however, if you move away from the relationship before you have learned the lesson. You may find it in another form down the road.

Your relationships are a tapestry of colors, geometric shapes, sounds, and vibrations. You come into a challenging relationship so you may transform your tapestry in a way that harmonizes with the shapes, colors, and sounds of the other person. This challenge is by design. The challenge is chosen by you to teach you about an aspect of you. If you end that relationship in search of another 'better one', it is as if you have selected to throw away the puzzle because it was too challenging, and you are now looking for a simpler puzzle. From our porch, we see you replacing puzzle after puzzle. It is, however, the part of you that you called the higher self who is continually bringing you, through synchronicity, those puzzles that you failed to complete. It is all scripted in your geometry and we can see it. We wish to tell you that it is all sacred.

You may move away from relationships when the lesson is learned. *How do we know that the lesson is learned?*, some may wonder. If you are miserable or angry, you still have work to do. It is when the relationship has taught you what it needed to, and you choose from a place of peace and neutrality to move away from it, that you have completed that puzzle and can begin a new one.

You are an angel and you come with another angel to learn about each other using the energy of love. There are great fluctuations to the energy of love and it is expressed through your emotions. Your emotions are the colors, paints, and textures you use to create your masterpiece. You are an artist and your relationship is your canvas. You apply your energy so the painting will carry you from one layer to the next. As you work and progress with your artwork, you develop mastery. The higher you get, the more transparent your creation becomes and therefore it reaches more people. The ripple becomes larger and larger. You must conquer the personal first in order to affect the whole. Your greatest challenge is often also your biggest gift. We ask you to hold sacred your relationships and to honor those who cross your path so they can help you learn about yourself.

Now, however, we wish to speak of the other side of relationships. We wish to touch upon those relationships that no longer support growth of either you or your partner. We wish to speak of relationships that no longer offer learning to either of you. It is when your relationship has reached a place of no heart connection or emotional interaction that you may contemplate ending it.

You come with another angel through contract. Both of you sign with a golden pen to work through the issues and challenges, using love. As you move through the layers, you must face many other emotions, such as anger, hate, jealousy, resentment, etc. You work through these other layers in order to clear them so you can eventually connect through love. The value of the relationships lies in the emotions. Your emotions are the fuel that propels you forward. If there is very little emotional energy exchange, you may not be able to move anywhere. The emotional exchange in your relationship, whether you perceive it as positive or negative, is your indication of your place in the lesson. It is when one of you, or both, stops caring about the relationship that you may find it is the right time to complete the puzzle and move to the next. Relationships require both parties to play the game. If one chooses to not play, then the other must allow it to end. One cannot play alone. It is in the exchange that learning is achieved.

We love you and we wish you to learn to feel which relationship offers you a fertile ground for growth and which relationship offers you no lesson. We wish you to understand that your journey is about you learning all aspects of "you." Your relationships are your mirrors, reflecting you back to you. It is when the mirror is no longer reflecting that you have an indication the lesson is about to end. When your partner no longer connects with you through emotions and feelings, the mirror is not doing its task of reflection.

Whatever you choose, you are honored and your free choice is sacred. You are a light being and those who read this message are in the forefront of a rapidly shifting planet. Your mission is to spread the light to those who are in the dark. We ask you to use your feeling from a place of peace and love. We ask you to find the fulcrum point in you, where you maintain balance. We wish you to evaluate your relationship from that place of neutrality and decipher if indeed it serves your path or not. Whatever you choose, know that there is no judgment and you are dearly loved, and so be it.

The Runway

I T IS AS IF IT HAPPENED YESTERDAY, some of you say to yourselves. You are surprised that time flows the way it does. There are those of you who feel as if they are chasing after time, but can never catch up. Many of you view time as liquid, and when you try to grasp it, it leaks between your fingers and is absorbed by the soil.

Why, some may ask, *are we having these issues with time?* Time is your runway, is our reply. You are like airplanes. You have a stretch that is limited in length and you must take off within the limits of the runway. Intuitively, you know that your mission is to take flight. You came to earth so you could come back up. Off course, in our dimension there is neither up nor down. We are with you, standing beside you, but you cannot see us because we are vibrating at a different rate. When you take flight, you can feel us, because there are those of us who blow the air that allows you to lift yourself above your current reality. Time is an illusion, and intuitively you know that it is. You come from a dimension of eternity to a dimension of time. Within the limits of time, you must learn to move yourself from one place to another. There is never a judgment and those who fly are as loved as those who do not. We must tell you, however, that the vista is beautiful from above.

We wish to tell you that the feeling accompanying a flying angel is one of love and peace. There are those of you who feel that time is there so they can get things done. They have a schedule every day, and they note in their calendar how to fill up every moment, so they will get from point A to point B. With all love, we wish to tell you that the destination is the letter Z. Getting from point A to B is achieved through a structured, well-designed life. To get to the letter Z, you must be in a place of miracles and allow trust and intuition to lead you. You must connect to the feminine side of you, as it represents your link to the natural elements around you. You must be at a place of not knowing, so you may feel. Only through surrendering to the higher part of yourself do you allow trust and feeling to show you the path. It is through the feelings of love and compassion that you gain higher velocity towards the end of the runway.

To get to the letter that represents the point of departure from the runway liftoff, you must use your tools. *Again tools!* , some of you may sigh. As we smile to you with so much love, we know how tired you are. We wish to let you know that you are eternal and that you have done it before.

It is our intention to explore with you some ways to achieve liftoff. You have a limited amount of time and many of you believe that by doing so much and cramming your schedules, you will get to the point where time will stop flowing and you will have it accumulated in your jar of linear perception. We wish to hold your hand while we take you from your place of seeing to spirit's place of seeing. Often, spirit's way of operating is counterintuitive.

From our seats, time is your friend and teacher. You designed this aspect of your lesson so you might experience continuous change. There are those of you who wish to stop time. For many of you, time is an enemy and therefore change is something to dread. Many of you try to appear younger. In your culture, youth is praised and old aged is looked upon as something to fear. We wish to tell you that many of you have it reversed. Time is your greatest companion, because it makes you shift your perception of who you are. **Time is your teacher, because it serves as a hint to the fact that you are not your body. As you grow old, many of you still feel young and many of you do not match inside what they see in the mirror. You are eternal and time is designed to give you clues to your eternity. You are born and within a short period of time** you reach old age. That span of time is your runway. Your greatest, most profound life portion is in the end portion of the runway, where you hopefully gathered enough speed so that your wings take flight.

Many of you look down at yourselves and see the body instead of looking at the spirit within. You have it reversed, and your culture reinforces your perception that youth is the time to take flight. We wish to hug and to love you as we repeat that there is never a judgment to when, where, and how you move in your lesson. The journey is from you to you. You are eternal and as soon as you return home, you laugh about those moments when you felt old. You then realize that the later years were the ones that had the canvas laid in front of you, the paint ready in front of you, and you also had the benefit of experience. You arrived at a place that artists dream of. You had the tools to paint and the understanding of the technique. You also had the vista wide open and mostly you had the time to paint.

As you mature, you begin to see those patterns in your life and they begin to make sense. As you grow beyond your youth, you begin to understand events that shook you earlier. As you progress, you begin to "see" the big picture and you are ready to begin the masterpiece, by connecting the dots. As you connect the dots, a circle emerges that is your true image. You are a vibration and your vibration with maturity has the capacity for more harmony and alignment with the universal resonance. It is by design.

Time is your friend, as it keeps you in an environment that is ever-changing, so you can learn, at every moment, about you. It is as if you are standing in a room and a lamp is lighting you from one side. That side is your youth. As you turn around slowly, the lamp illuminates a different aspect of you. Why would you not want to see one aspect and care only for the other? All aspects of you are beautiful and sacred.

We see you like you really are. You appear to us like a swirl of energy cluster that shifts and changes. You are like a galaxy with awesome colors around you. You carry a melody and it changes, too, according to your state. You are like an event and you are a magnificent sight. We can see in you your tests, your experiences, and your challenges. You are truly a piece of what you call God. *If I am so beautiful, why don't I see it when I look at the mirror?*, some of you may ask. We wish you to replace the mirror that you are using and use our mirror. *Can we buy one?*, some of you may joke. You have one. It is through looking with your feeling center that you begin to see your true nature. When you see yourself from the vantage point of your eternity, you begin to see the sacredness of every stage of your life. Many of you miss opportunities and miss the beautiful vista that comes to them in the later part of their lives.

We are in love with you and as we hold your hands, we see that the geometry around your body changes. The change is not because you aged, but because you begin to "feel bad" about your body as it ages. We must impart to you who develop negative feelings toward your vessel that your body will honor your wishes and will become as you see it, negative. You are the creator of your mirror. You are here not only to learn about yourself as youth. You are here to learn about yourself and honor yourself at every stage of your life. It is, however, the later part that holds the greatest reward.

We wish to speak to you about taking flight. You are on the runway and you are gathering speed. Many of you in your culture dread the end of the runway, because they see it as the end of their life. We know who you are and you are built for survival. It is, however, the end of the runway that brings you to a place where you can ascend. As you get nearer the end of the runway, you become less dense. So much so that you can shift your dimension and defy physical death. This is how glorious the end of the runway is.

It is, however, the point that so many of you begin to feed yourselves with the idea that the best is behind you.

We see many of you fold your wings toward the end of the runway and choose only to look back with nostalgia to the beginning of the runway. We love you and there is no judgment as to how you see your airplane and whether you take flight or stay down. We wish to tell you that those of you who are guided to receive this information are those who were meant to take off at the end of the runway. You are built to ascend higher than you were allowed in the past. The magnetic fields around you limited many of you on your past journey. This is now changing, and your runway stretches to become longer. Your velocity is increasing as well. You stood in line to be here so you could fly. We wish you to do just that.

How do we do it?, you may ask. Your speed is connected to the way you view yourself. It is connected to the love you have for yourself. Only when you are honoring yourself and your vehicle are you poised to move upward. We wish you to embrace time as your greatest teacher. We wish you to look backward with neutrality and we wish you to view the future with neutrality. Only when you find neutrality with the past and the future do you truly discover being in the now. Now is your only true reality.

We can see your perception of time in your geometry. As you begin to truly live in the now, the triangles around your physical body shift and become circular. Your melody becomes harmonious and the stars surrounding you sparkle like the stars in the desert night sky. It is truly a sight to watch. You are dearly loved, whether you fly or not.

There are those of you who are here at this time to be the ones who hold a vibration that allows the planet to shift to a higher place. They are called the place holders. We know who you are. You are meant to be the ones who take off at the end of the runway, so the rest of humanity can see the vista from above through you.

Many of you, at this time, are in the middle of the runway and we see you looking at your vehicles and asking yourselves, *how can I fly with this?* With all love, we ask you to not stop at this point. This is why you came down, so you can take off. You are more enabled than ever before in your history as human on this planet. We ask that you enjoy this ride, because it is the reason you came here.

As you pass through time, it is not what you do that matters; it is how you feel while doing what you do that takes you upward. We wish you to live your life knowing that you are eternal and loved, so every moment will offer you a wonder. We wish you to slow down, so you can sense your breath and your heartbeat. We love you and we wish to fly beside you as you take off at the end of the runway, and so be it.

Drinking Nectar

YOU HAVE COME THUS FAR. When we see you, we can also see your history. We can see where you came from. Some of you have come from vast distances to be here at this time of change on this planet. There are those of you who have traveled from the other side of your universe to be here at this time. This is a time of celebration and everyone wanted to be at the graduation party.

What do we have to celebrate?, you may wonder. *Can you tell us why should we be happy? It looks so bad out there, how can we celebrate many of you ask?* We wish you to celebrate because you are alive during the most momentous moment of change in your history as a human walking in duality on this planet, is our short answer. **You did not come here at this time to be lying in your hammocks, drinking the nectar of heaven. You are the transformers of energy. You are built to bring light to where it is dark. You are the one who trained for this time and dreamt of the opportunity to be here when it all happens. Those of you who are hearing these messages, we ask you to please remember who you are and wake up, because you are the warriors of light. Do**

you think that you came here to rest? We have news for you.
This is your time to shine. This is the defining hour and
it is your opportunity to make a difference for the whole.
So many angels at this time are walking in their day to
day wrapped in a blanket that keeps them from seeing
who they are. So many angels are in darkness, experiencing life as a constant challenge and drama without seeing
the beauty of it. You are the one who came here at this
time to light your candle so others could see. We wish to
tell you that this is your time. That is why we ask you to
celebrate. What you trained for, for millennia, is actually
happening now and you want to sit this one out? We love
you and we wish you to wake up to your purpose, because
the time is now.

Like a doctor who wishes to heal people, you went to
school for many years. Finally, you got the certificate and
you must choose what to do with it. We wish to tell you
that you have worked very hard to be here at this time
with the knowledge and the experience that you have. So
much planning went into the timing of your birth. So
much planning and coordination went into choosing your
parents, siblings, friends, and challenges. All your experiences up until now prepared you to be poised at the right
place and the right time so you could make a difference.
Why would the doctor choose not to heal people after
all this training? When the student becomes a doctor,
he gets a certificate that he is ready to do the work. He

is ready to make a difference in the lives of people. You are that doctor. Throughout your many lives you were trained, so the accumulated experience of all your past expressions will bring you to the forefront at this time.

You are here and now by choice and by design. We hug you and we love you, whether you fulfill your mission or not. We can tell you, for certain, that you are trained for it. We wish to remind you how excited you were before descending to this plane called earth. You were so thrilled that you would have a shot at making a difference. We wish to tell you that now is the time. *Okay, some of you may say. Although we are tired, we understand that we need to wake up, but we are not sure what to do.* We wish to tell you that you always begin with intention. You must begin by asking to be shown what it is that you need to know and do. It is in the intensity of your intent that your path will be opened to you, like the flower that blooms when it is time. You are ready and you carry in your memory and your cells all the knowledge needed to do your work. You have the akashic records available to you, so you may access all the lives and experiences from your past expressions.

I am tired, many of you whisper as you read these sentences. We must impart to you that you feel tired only when you are removed from your purpose. When you move aimlessly on your path, you are tired. It is when you give intent to move onto your mission that you become tireless. When you move away from the structure and into the inter-dimensionality of your existence, life becomes exciting. When you wake up to your mission, the tiredness dissipates and you are so excited that you cannot sleep at night. It is we who love you and who are keeping you awake at night, so we can celebrate together.

What do I do after giving intent?, some of you may wonder. The intent is the car that can take you places. Now you must put fuel in the car. The fuel is your willingness to allow change in your life. When you came to the planet, you agreed to forget why you came. It is you who then must form other ideas of why you came, and many of them are based on your environment. You have your parents, school, religion, and government institutions telling you what it is that you need to become. Then you have the media, which tells you what you need to think, what you should have, and how you should look when you do what you do. There is much that you need to clear from your perception. You must begin to allow that which forms you to disintegrate, so the real purpose of your journey can emerge. For that, you must allow change.

You want to tell me that I have to throw away everything that I worked for?, some may ask in fear. It is exactly what we are asking you to do. We are asking you to throw away the fear that you have worked so hard to build. We are asking you to let go of those things that keep you under control of others and become free. Yes, we do ask you to take down the walls that you built, so love can re-enter your life and you will be present enough so you may feel it. We ask you to take down the walls of prejudices, so you may begin to experience love rather than hate for those who are different from you.

You are beautiful and for you to feel the magnificence of you, you must be willing to change. You must be willing to let go of all the darkness, so you can begin to shine your light. You have been sold on many things and those things act as a blanket that obscures your light. You must be ready to change and remove all the layers that keep your light from shining.

What will become of me?, some of you may wonder. *I am afraid that I will not recognize myself. I am afraid that I will lose everything.* As we hug you and hold your hands, we wish to tell you that indeed you will. You will lose many things that hold you from flying. You may lose your fear; you may lose your anger. You may even lose your resentment and jealousies. You may lose your drama. You may gain, however, other things that are built inside of you and are just waiting to be found.

What could that be?, some of you may wonder. As you move away from anger, you find love; as you move from separation, you find unity; as you move from hate, you find compassion; and as you move from drama, you find peace. Do you think you are ready to move from drama and settle with peace? Can you afford to lose hate and replace it with compassion? Can you fathom being at a place of light, where darkness is fearful to be in your vicinity, because it too will transform? This is the second step and we ask you to not fear it, because all you have to lose is that which keeps you chained and all you need to gain is that which allows you to fly.

So what should I expect then?, some may wonder yet again. You can expect that everything in your life will begin to shift. You will begin to feel that nothing is what it seems and everything in your life, that you once believed was one thing, turns out to be another. This portion is exciting and it is your perception of reality that is shifting inside of you and it is being reflected back to you. It is not that your life will fall apart, but it is your perception of what is around you that will change to the extent that it will feel as if everything is collapsing. This is, my dear angel, a step that allows the old to be cleared so the new can come in. You can't hold on to heaviness if you wish to fly. As heaviness transforms, it must pass through you and out. For when it passes through you, you must acknowledge it and feel it.

There are angels who begin to wake up and all of a sudden they become fearful of all the darkness they see. They are horrified and they wish they never started. We wish to tell you that the darkness was there all along, but now that you begin to shine your light, the darkness inside of you is exposed. Once exposed, it must transform. When you see the darkness, it is because it was always there and now is the time to let go of it as well. When you do, it may feel awful, because you must process it one last time before it leaves you forever. When you do, you may release heaviness that has accumulated over many of your past expressions. This experience can be intense and many of you will not understand why this is happening. We love you so for walking the walk. We wish to tell you to be patient and loving with yourself. Forgive yourself for the things you have done in your past lives, so you can become lighter. Some of you become angry. You feel that the spiritual path is a con. You feel that you were betrayed. You asked for peace and you have found more anger than you ever experienced. We wish to impart to you that it is part of the process and it is essential. You must clear the dark before you move to the light. The spiritual exposes what you have been hiding. Embrace that which is ugly and love it as it is a part of you as well.

There is never a judgment as you are on a journey of learning the different aspects of yourself. Those aspects are at times difficult and you must come to peace with them as well. We tell you over and over that the most important attribute on this path is to love yourself, as you are parts and pieces of God walking in duality. When you use love with all of your different aspects, your divinity is revealed and you take the hand of spirit and walk the path that you intended to walk. You are the light warriors and this is your battle. Do not fear it as you have all the tools in your possession and you have trained for it for millennia. This is the time to use your divinity and light as a bridge for humanity to walk on, so peace on earth will come. With love, we bid you goodbye for now, although we never leave. We ask you to wake up to your appointment, and so be it.

END OF PART 1

Message Guide

1. You have, over millennia, moved away from your emotions and feelings, discarding them as feminine or irrational. You have moved away from the divine, feminine side of yourselves to the rational, masculine side. By doing so, you have created imbalance within yourselves and your relationships to the planet (p6) "The Buffet"

2. You are experiencing a shift of paradigm. This shift manifests on all levels of consciousness and therefore it is expressed through your biology as well. You are becoming more enabled than ever as a human. It is a wonderful time to smell the flowers, to slow down and "feel" your selves. (p6)

3. When you do what you deeply desire and are passionate about it, the energy you transmit is powerful. When you choose to do something that is a "compromise" in order to meet your responsibilities and make ends meet, it is as if you were, from our perspective, attempting to drive a fast new car without fuel. You are pushing the car with your hands or legs while trying to move forward. (p12) "Car Without Fuel"

4. If you were wondering why many of you who "act responsibly" and "do the right thing" for the benefit of your families or communities feel so depressed and joyless, then understand that without passion your actions do not carry

the joy that you know you can feel. It is through the energy that you create, while doing the things that fulfill you the most, that you make music. (p12)

5. It is our intention to help you realize your full potential by guiding you through the mechanism of spirit. From our perspective it is simple. You have two main tools and the rest is a variation on this theme. The first is love, and the second is intent. These two are the vehicle and the fuel. (p17) "Small Holding cell"

6. It is by design that you have been programmed not to trust your feelings. There are those who operate in the shadow of darkness who wish to harness your emotional energy. This is very valuable to them. Like you, they use it as energy to propel themselves. You have been diverted to move away from your emotions, to doubt your emotions, to control your emotions, and to learn to re-direct your emotions. These are all campaigns of manipulation to steer you away from your truth. (p17)

7. There are many who wish to block your vision. They spend vast resources to create an environment that diverts you from the true picture. This environment is embedded with frequencies of fear that hold you like an anchor in the harbor so you cannot sail to the open sea. (p21) "Earth's Sister Planet"

8. From where we stand, who you are has nothing to do with what you do, how much you have, or your social statues. (p25) "A Farmer in Northern China"

9. We do not distinguish between rich and poor, nor do we relate differently to those who have more social influence, political power, or outer beauty. From the side we are standing on, these are external roles you came to play in order to grow and learn. (p25)

10. From where we stand, there are no arbitrary lessons. All your experiences are planned and executed perfectly for your learning. (p27)

11. We want you to know that those daily life scenes you were crying on or laughing at and those scenes that made you cringe or smile are events produced for you in the world of "spirit-Hollywood" so you can grow spiritually and evolve. (p31) "The Movie Theater"

12. By discovering the light within you, you pass the test, you change everything. We wish to tell you that your feelings are your tools. Use them appropriately and you will have access to the most powerful treasure on earth: you (p32)

13. As you walk in your body contemplating life and going through your day, you have an enormous support group. You have your cells, your higher selves, and then there are others. You may call them angels or guides. They are part

of you, yet separated. They are the link between you and your higher you. They also translate some of the messages from your cells, injecting thoughts into you so you may consider alternatives. (p37) "The Different 'Yous'"

14. When you signed up for the role, a contract was signed. All of the "yous" were there to sign. The contract read that within the sacred mission of coming to earth and living the cycle you call life, your wishes will be honored regardless if they are respectful to your biology, life, or Gaia. Your choices will be honored and respected without judgment. (p38)

15. You are not different at all. You are like us, an angelic energy whose purpose is to become one through creation. (p40)

16. There are some of us who wish to read you the instructions as you walk and act. We wish to hold your hands, and we do. But it is you who must want to learn the new skills. It is you who needs to ask for our guidance. There is a universal law on this planet: free choice. Your choice is honored without judgment. If you wish to use the manual, you will find that your life becomes easier, more joyous, and more balanced. (p43) "The Magic Manual"

17. It is your intention that will set you down the correct path. If your intention is to fool yourself, you will indeed do that. You are a master in disguise. You can pretend to be a human, a victim, or the one who is led by circumstances. (p44)

18. You are built to fight for life and to fear death. You are built for survival. It is ironic to us that many of you are in survival mode, trying so hard to stay alive, and at the same time do not honor the life of others and of earth. (p47) "The Air That You Breath"

19. Many religions have tried to convince you that you need to be part of the structure to experience love. From our perspective, that is as valid as asking you to pay for the air that you breathe. (p51)

20. The feeling of loneliness is from the connection to you. You have abandoned yourself. Many of you have followed your costumes and believed in your roles, only to find that the role did not carry substance. Some of you looked elsewhere for the eternal beautiful substance that makes you who you are. Many of you have pursued the wrong treasure or a false one. This process was a test. Some of you have followed whatever looked the shiniest and did not look at the brightest jewel of all, the one hiding inside of you. (p54) "Open The Bag"

21. When you walk feeling lonely, you are in darkness. When you feel not loved, you are in darkness. It is not an evil attribute. It is the attribute of an angel who lost touch with its divinity. Darkness is a cut between you and you. The more you separate from yourself, the darker shade you take. (p57)

22. All the aspects of the "arbitrary people," who seemingly popped into your life, are aspects of you who came to introduce themselves so you will know more about yourself. (p64)

23. We want to hold your hand so you can slow down. You think that if you move faster, you will get somewhere and can then relax. It as if the hamsters will arrive sooner by spinning on the carousel more quickly. We wish you to enjoy the ride. You have done many of these cycles before, but this one is for the record. (p68) "Change In The Final Act"

24. You and your body are teammates. You share the same goal and you come together to work as one. It is indeed a sacred union that you have with the group that you call your body. Would you treat your teammate with disrespect before an important game? Would you give your teammate the wrong sports shoes to wear before that big game? (p71) "You And Your Body Are Teammates"

25. When you begin the spiritual process we call ascension, you require energy. The process of ascension has to do with moving away from your karma or your groove and charting a new, magnificent path. (p74)

26. If you feel that something is wrong for you, then it is. Listen to your body, watch it, observe it, and love it like you love your favorite teammate. Your body will respond. It is not the food that makes the greatest difference; it is the in-

tention. As you listen and pay attention, you tell your body that it matters. You renew your vows and let it know that you are committed to your partnership. Your body will respond. (p74)

27. The love of spirit is such that even though you feel that there's only darkness around you, you are still loved. Even when you create darkness in your daily life, the light inside of you is always there waiting for you to choose it. Such is the love of spirit. It is always available to hug you at any moment. (p76) "The Pilot Light"

28. Many of you are so afraid to let go of the "bad" feelings because it feels so familiar. We know who you are. You have ground yourselves for so many lives—smelling the dirt, being abused, being hurt, betrayed, punished, prosecuted, executed—that you feel at home with being a victim. (p77)

29. What used to work in the past will no longer work as well. The swirling of energy will not leave anything where it was. This energy is the energy of ascension and it is powerful. It takes you upward on a journey that requires trust and fearlessness. (p82) "The Old And The New"

30. The old energy has to do with the energy of control. It is also the energy of fear. The old energy is wrapped in manipulation. Many of the old energy ways have to do with channeling you to do something that does not serve you, so you will not "see" who you are. In the old energy, you had

to have everything translated so you could understand true from false. In the new energy, you do not need translations as you will observe that false sounds like false and truth will harmonize with you. (p86)

31. GOD is outside your sensory ability. God's form exists beyond your perception and so you take that perfect circle and you chop it up so it will fit your reality. You build concepts, names, and ideas; on top of those you build ideologies, structures, hierarchies; at the top of everything you crown GOD as the ruler. (p90) "Bread Crumbs On The Forest Floor"

32. We hug you and we wish to tell you about one of the most important attributes of GOD. GOD is the essence of LOVE. It is the kind of love that never judges, never punishes, and never asks anything from you. It is LOVE and it is there always inside of you waiting to be discovered. (p90)

33. All the good and bad that some may attribute to GOD is your choice; the choice of the God portion of you, which directs your lessons this time around. The evil and darkness you encounter in your life is just a manifestation of your free choice. This is part of the test you have designed; "with free choice, what will you choose light or dark?" (p93)

34. When we love you, it is not because of your diamonds or cars or pretty faces. We do not even register that. We see

you as pure energy. We see you the way you are, an angel, a piece of God. When we hug you we do not feel your fur coat or your designer outfit. We hug your heart; we embrace your soul. It is the physical costume that we do not register. That is our blind spot. We just see what you do with what you have. (p97) "The Big Boss"

35. There are those who choose not to use sexual energy. From our perspective, it is like using a car but taking out the engine. Sexual energy is the most powerful energy source you possess. The destination is your own choice. Those who choose to remove that energy from their lessons will have to walk rather then use the fast car they have been given. (p101)

36. You think that you are being moved like a marionette. Some of you believe that others control your actions regardless of your wishes. When we tell you that you are powerful, it is because you are the creator. The need and ability to create is an innate part of who you are and it is your birthright. When you are without a body on this dimension, all you do is create. (p103) "Like A Marionette"

37. You contain all you need, and you create what you need when you are in the now. When you are walking hand in hand with your breath, feeling your heartbeat, you are powerful. The joy comes from being you with you. (p107)

38. If you could peek into the crystal ball and know your future, it would mean that the future holds the answers and therefore the answers are not held by you. You are the master of your path, always. (p111) "The Crystal Ball"

39. As you move, the colors around you change, the geometric forms that you create change, the melody that you create changes, and everything around you responds to the changes in you. As you act, you create a domino effect. You find that love and peace changes the future for you and for the planet. (p112)

40. Even at that time in the desert, you had the power to create abundance. You are powerful in every environment. Your power to create is not dependent on the landscape; it comes from within. As you trust, you manifest trust. When you fear, you manifest fear. As you focus on survival, you will create the circumstances in which survival will be needed. (p113)

41. As you walk the planet in your biology, even in the darkest places your inner light is showing you the path. You cannot get lost anymore unless you choose to. The results of your walk do become apparent as you walk. It is not about the future. Your path is about walking moment by moment in a certain vibration. (p117) "Opening The Lockbox"

42. There are many of you who fear enablement because you do not want to know. You feel that knowing is too heavy.

We say to you with all love that there is no judgment on you whether you choose to see or not. You are loved just the same. We know who you are. There are those of you who opened your lockbox in previous cycles and were burnt at the stake or tortured for carrying your light. You carry within you a cellular fear that activates your survival mode whenever you reach to that box. (p118)

43. There are many who feel that they do not want or are unable to change, and they want to find a way to get off the planet so they can come back more equipped as indigos. There is no judgment, but why would you want to miss the fireworks celebration? This is the most exciting of times on your planet. (p119)

44. The most important step in moving to a higher frequency is self-love. It is not what you call being egocentric. Self-love is void of ego. It is the profound understanding that you are one with the universe and you are made of the essence of love. It is the understanding that all life is connected by invisible strings, and when you hurt other life you are in actuality hurting your self. (p125) "Your Brothers And Sisters"

45. The imbalance of the planet manifests in viruses and bacteria. It also manifests in food that has no love essence in it, which actually causes your body to create allergies. It also manifests in destructive forces of nature that attempt to preserve the balance by purging and cleansing parts of

itself. It is the same with your body. Cancer is the attribute of a disconnection between you and you. When you understand that you are part of God and you are part of all creation, you have no choice but to love yourself. (p125)

46. Through orgasm you reach into hyperspace for a moment and you experience the melting of all the yous into one. It is as if all of the yous that are playing their part have been spiraled into one vessel. It is from our perspective the highest vibration you can reach with your current awareness. It is why we love you and urge you to make peace with yourself and make peace with your body—to love yourself and honor your body, so you and your body can co-create the spiral of ascension. (p128) "Orgasm As A State Of Being"

47. You have been programmed to limit this vibration to your genitals, thereby reducing the power of it to mere seconds. The orgasm is a state of being. It is a vibration that your cells were meant to experience for a prolonged period of time. You are enabled to carry this vibration as you walk on your street and we can assure you that you will be smiling. (p132)

48. At times you feel that you are living in a race of sorts for time. In order to win the race, you must achieve those things that your culture tells you that you should have. It is when you achieve all that you have been sold on, that you discover the real story. You discover that you are no better

than you were before you had all these things. (p137) "The Race"

49. Your story is much vaster than the one you have been sold on. You came here to transform your planet and the universe, and instead you spend your energy trying to live up to an image that is based on what you wear, where you work, how you look, and how much you make. Does that sound divine to you? (p138)

50. You are vibrating instruments. To yourselves, you appear solid, but to us you are a vibration. We see you in terms of your colors, we see you in term of your light, we see you in terms of the shapes that surround you, and we can hear your melody. You are a giant orchestra and pyrotechnic display, combined. You are beautiful to us; you are magnificent in every way. (p142) "I Want To Go Back"

51. You come and go and each time you choose the most appropriate costume to fit your lesson. There are no mistakes. You put great effort into choosing the right outfit. Way more effort goes into choosing your body than all the time you have been choosing clothes to fit your body. (p143)

52. It is the mastery of communication that will change the way you talk to one another. We see it between couples. One speaks one thing, and the other hears something completely different. It is because one speaks words and the other "hears" the vibrations. (p151) "You Are Transparent"

53. Things are changing, and you need to become one with you. When your vibration is split from your expression, when you do one thing but mean another, you cause splitting in yourself. You send the message of splitting to your cells, and they respond to your vibration and express it as disease. (p152)

54. There will be a time, not in the far future, when you may be tested. You will be shown a frequency meant to freeze you and send you to hide your light in the corner. It is then that you will need to use all of your power of discretion to separate truth from falsehood not based on the reports from the news, but on the reports from between your eyebrows. (p152)

55. You have a body; your body is an instrument. It does things for you. It serves you. At times, as we look at you, we feel that you serve your body instead of asking your body to serve you. Your body is your sacred heritage. It is your most precious gift. Without it, you cannot exercise your lesson on the planet. Some of you are surprised, then, when your body fails you. (p154) "Sacred Heritage"

56. Did you know that your cells sing? Yes, they have a tone that can be harmonious or disharmonious. When your cells sing songs out of tune, you may take on cancer as a manifestation of the discord. You are the most evolved species on this planet and yet you are the only one that knowingly and intentionally self-destructs. (p157)

57. When you place the chickens in a darkened room with bad air and no place to move around, inject them with growth hormones, antibiotics, and bad food and still expect them to give you food that will support your biology, you are deluding yourselves. They are just honoring your choice and giving you back what you ask them to give you. (p158)

58. The love force, as we call it, has the power to create suns and stars. It is even in what you call a black hole. It is the context of matter and antimatter. Most importantly to you, it surges in your veins. Your cells, each and every one, carry that thing you call love. (p161) "Love It Is Then"

59. When you are in love, the substance that your glands secrete actually opens a door, which inter-dimensionally is a vortex that connects you to that love force of which you become part. When you are "in love," you are feeling the vibration that is most prevalent in the universe and in creation. (p161)

60. Darkness is not represented by the seemingly "bad" things that happen in your life. Those "things" are part of your lesson. They are either karmic setups or the choices you have made to facilitate your own growth. Those actual events in your life that you see as negative, terrible, horrific, and sad are not darkness. It is the response to those events that represent either light or dark. (p167) "Dark and Light"

61. All souls who committed the most heinous crime knew of their appointments. It is in the synchronicity of events in which one lesson and one karma intersect and manifest to create learning on both sides. Both the victim and the perpetrator in all violent crimes, as arbitrary as they may seem, were there by appointment. Your life planning is precious and sacred. Your journey is followed by many of us who are waiting for you to reach out and ask for guidance. Do you think then that people would just drop dead and for some reason that was not planned? (p169)

62. We wish to tell you that storms will come, as it is part of the shifting of energy. The new replaces the old. When the transition takes place one must leave so the other can move in its place. There will be a lot of movement. It is spiritual and it is appropriate. We wish to tell you how to recognize that you are indeed the one who was assigned a lighthouse. (p176)

63. When those things that happen in the world seem scary, know deep inside that you were built for this mission. You are a lighthouse and you are powerful. This is why you came here at this time and no storm can hurt you. This is when you will feel that you are full. You will know that you are in the right place at the right time. There will be no more questions. Do you ever want to miss such an honor? (p178) "Get Out Of Bed"

64. It is by the weight of things that you can measure their energy and their meaning for you. When something feels heavy, it means that it pulls energy away from you; therefore, it may have a negative implication on your life. When you feel light, it means that you are receiving energy and that is a sign that you are in the positive. (p183) "Heavy Or Light"

65. Do not judge the others as each one of you is on a different path and, therefore, what you call your "truth" may differ. At times, two angels will use two directly opposite approaches to reach the same treasure. Do not judge your friends, for what is good for them may not be good for you and vice versa. (p184)

66. From our perspective, truth is not linear or singular. On a spiritual path there are as many truths as there are angels. One of the attributes of the new energy is that you must learn to honor each other's belief systems, traditions, and words. Those traditions are about intent and about you. It does not matter if you use this prayer or that prayer. It does not matter if you chant this mantra or that mantra. It is about you connecting with you. (p185)

67. Often it is the opposite: By asking and receiving that which does not serve your path, you go backward and find that the more you have the less you feel. The more you acquire, the less you have time to enjoy. The more you have, the more separated from your family and people you be-

come. The more you have, the less happy you become. You asked for more and more, and because you are the creator of your reality, that which you ask for will manifest. (p190) "Wait a Minute"

68. You are the creator. If you believe that you can only create something small, that is exactly what you will manifest. How about asking to be shown the way to your highest potential and to your most glorious path and forgo the specifics? How about trusting that the universe knows your highest potential? (p191)

69. We are in love with you and we wish to tell you that you can only co-create with spirit for which you have intended. When you ask for our hand, know that you will be shown the way, as your higher-self begins to change the plans and to coordinate new plans which will serve your life the best and lead you to your highest potential.When your life changes, do not say, Wait a minute! I just wanted the rent to be paid, but I do not want to change my life for that. (p192)

70. You think that things just happen. Well, next time we ask that you celebrate that which is seemingly a coincidence, because so much planning goes into it. All day long you are being directed. You call these things accidents or coincidences. You get frustrated when you are stuck is traffic. You curse often when the place that you intended to go to closed just as you arrived. We love you and we know who you are. You are an angel walking blindfolded, thinking that every-

thing around you just happens. Next time, when you are in traffic and your car is not moving, why don't you celebrate it? (p197) "The Traffic Jam"

71. The mechanics of your guide's messages move from light to heavy and from the subtle to the gross. It is when you do not react to the subtle message that the follow-up is heavier, and so it goes. When you get a painful message, you may want to look back and examine the signs that were there, but you missed them because you were too busy moving around. (p199)

72. There is a greater story out there. The story is in the circle. You are always searching for answers. Many of the answers are in front of you. Most of you can't see them because you look in straight lines, but the answers are in the circle. It is the story of the three-dimensional reality versus the multidimensional reality. Explaining multidimensional reality to a human is like explaining to a fish how to ride a bicycle. It is a different reality; so much so, that the only way for us to describe it is through metaphors. Although metaphors do not tell the real story, they convey the feeling. (p202) "A Fish Riding A Bicycle"

73. You are on the eve of a new era. It is you who chose to vibrate higher and change your future. Your future was a probability, and you have chosen a different probability, a truly grand one, and you are on track to graduate. We wish to impart to you that your time, as you know it, is collaps-

ing. You are experiencing an acceleration of time as you know it. What it means is that various dimensions are colliding and you will begin to experience multiple realities simultaneously. (p205)

74. It is a choice and we must tell you that there are those who wish to stay with the reality of the old. They may not experience the shift and collapse of time the way you do. They might experience fear and create a reality very different from the one we are describing. As dimensions collapse into each other, there may be more than one reality on the playing field. One reality can be called heaven, and the other may be called hell. One may experience despair and the other bliss. Both will be on earth in their bodies in this dimension and both will experience that which they choose. Their experiences, however, will be very different. (p207)

75. We know that it is not easy to be an old soul engaged in the new reality amidst younger souls engaged in the old reality. They do not question anything, because they are just excited to be around. They seem like they are having fun. A nagging feeling, however, weighs on you and keeps you awake at night. You know something profound is going on, so you do not understand how everyone around you sleeps like logs while you twist and turn. You wonder often about your sanity. Sometimes you even hear voices and you are not sure who it is talking to you. You turn to the left and you turn to the right, and there is no one. Then you think to yourself, I hope no one noticed. (p209) "The Cell Phone"

76. You think you are the only one, but there are many of you old souls working the trenches in places where the light is very dim. They are doing what you are doing. They are acting as vessels to channel the frequency that allows the spiritual attributes of the planet to change. You are doing inter-dimensional work by keeping your light on. It is a sacred work and you have a group the watches you and supports you day and night. (p211)

77. We know that you are tired. We wish to tell you that this is your battle. You are in the midst of it. Your mission, as a light warrior, is to hold your light. Your mission is to find peace inside of you despite the turmoil that is all around you. Do you see why you need to be with people and not in the mountains? The mountains do not need your light; other humans need it. This is how you change the planet: one drop at a time. Who do you think will do the job, GOD? We love you and we wish to tell you that GOD it is. (p213)

78. As time moves faster, you must learn to slow down so you will stay in balance. Your biological clock will be ticking at the same rate, but your perception will be that you are slowing down. It is because everything around you will move faster. We know it is confusing, but you are about to enter a confusing time in which your logical mind will be stretched and challenged. (p215) "There Has Never Been A Better Time"

79. Many of you fear the feeling of lightness. You fear being happy because you suspect it. If you are happy, something will go wrong and will show you that it was just temporary. Many of you carry memories of times in past cycles when you were happy and then everything changed and the happiness was taken away from you. So many of you hold back on your lives because the thought of experiencing happiness terrifies you. As long as you feel in a slump, you know where you are and feel comfortable with it. (p216)

80. We wish you to tell yourself that the time is now. There is no tomorrow, only the now. Do not wait for the opportunity in the future. Many of you give yourselves excuses for why it is difficult to move away from heaviness. It is true that gravity pulls you down stronger the heavier you are. We ask you to become lighter so when you laugh, you really mean it, and when you tell your friends, I am happy, you really mean it. When you find the time to feel, it means that you stepped off the treadmill. (p217)

81. Light shows you all aspects of you. Part of these aspects are what you call positive and part is what you may consider negative. All of you carry that duality. Light has no judgment and it does not give you marks if you are good or bad. It shows you exactly what you are. You are asked at this time is to embrace both. (p223) "Not So Pretty"

82. The bad is a continuum of the good. Your journey is progressing within the spectrum of the same color. Most of

you are not all "good" and not all "bad." It is the learning that you came here to do. We ask you to stop judging yourselves and start loving yourselves. (p224)

83. You cannot say, I love my head but I hate my knees. It is you and you must take the whole package. Do not say, I was bad and now I am good. Say, I am an angel and I have divinity. The divinity was hidden before and now it is revealed. It was however always with me. It is now my intent to activate it in my life. (p228)

84. Some of us tend to be the creative artists. There are those among us who are masters of creation of biological forms on earth and elsewhere. We use energy in a precise way to create new ways for biological forms to develop and adapt. You call this process nature or evolution. We love you and we wish to tell you that we are part of that energy you call nature and evolution. It is not a blind process, but a process with consciousness. (p230) "What Do Angels Do?"

85. Many of you fear change. We know who you are. Before you come into your biology, you are eternal. Soon after coming into a body you forget your eternity and you worry about the changes. You are not used to change, because where you come from, you do not age. In biology, as soon as you get used to your face and body and become comfortable with yourself, you grow different. Time is a trickster and does not let you rely on physical appearance for your happiness. We know some of you who are in an advanced

age and feel and act like teenagers. (p237) "Changing Of The Guards"

86. Your fear of aging speeds up the aging process. When you acknowledge the limitation of your physical body and try to make it look the same as it was when you were a teenager, it is like keeping a good wine from aging. Since you only get better with age, why would you want to miss this process by trying to stay at the level you were in as a teenager? (p238)

87. When a human plants a seed of enlightenment, all around will begin to see the light. Light does not have an agenda. Light does not try to convince anyone of its attribute. Light just reveals what is there. (p240) "Shadowed Light"

88. We understand that you are built for survival, and some of you wish to maintain aspects of yourselves although it does not benefit you. The planet's energy is changing and that which is hidden must be revealed and exposed. It is your light that makes this happen. You will find those who operate with shadow very protective. They set up systems so that the light will not get too close. (p242)

89. Let us say that someone from an institution tells you that if you don't do something, then you will not be granted salvation by GOD. This assertion is an example of shadow. Shadow will often be expressed from a source of fear and

from an intention of instilling fear. Light, though, operates through choice and love. Whenever you are told that you must do something or the repercussion from spirit will be harsh, it is a shadow of fear that you are seeing. (p244)

90. Physical matter responds to the level of commitment that you invest in an idea. This commitment's intensity moves and translates energy into a miracle. Although in our reality all is vibration where miracles, as you call them, happen all the time, in your reality you made a commitment to linearity and reason, so whenever you desire that which does not comply with your linear thinking, you dismiss it as impossible. The molecules are aware of the intensity of your belief and the vibration arranges itself to fit your limitation. (p250) "The Magician"

91. We ask you to not hurry to accept that which the grown-ups or your institutions and governments tell you. You are the one who came to this beautiful planet to change that which you have been told cannot be changed. It is your belief in peace on earth that will bring miracle after miracle. We ask you to become childlike. (p252)

92. With all love, we ask you to go back to that magical place in your heart. Dust the old books about fairies and fantasies. Remember how it made you feel as a child. Now as you sit down on the floor, candle in front of you, apply this magic to the planet. The planet needs you at any age and you are loved no matter what you do. (p252)

93. We wish to impart to you, however, that those who walk in darkness beside you, while you walk in the sun, are part of your contract. If you choose not see the sun just so you can get closer to them, you are dishonoring them and your own path. (p267)

94. Many in your culture hold the belief that the soul enters the womb earlier. It is indeed correct that the soul enters the womb well before birth, but it travels back and forth. The soul enters the fetus before birth so it could harmonize with and adjust to the undeveloped brain. The soul contains a large energy field that is all-knowing, and the brain of a fetus is very primitive and constricted. It takes some tweaking and getting comfortable for this large energy to create the connection with the brain and allow the two frequencies to join and harmonize. It is not an easy task but you all did it. (p271) "The Lovers"

95. When there is no light, you cannot see, but your imagination works. There are those who create images in the dark. They do not see, because light is absent, but their ability to create remains. They are your brothers and sisters and they are divine like you. Like you they are family and they have the signature of GOD running in their veins. They are loved by spirit just like you. They are the ones who come, life after life, to be the balance of darkness in your planet of free choice. (p278) "Dracula"

96. You are part of the energy of the planet and your biology represents the macro of the planet. The planet represents the macro of the universe. Each part represents the infinite in small scale. For you to truly battle the light and dark inside of you, the planet needs to maintain that balance, and so does the universe. The dark is a part of you as much as the light. It is the energy that makes you who you are, walking in duality in lesson. (p280)

97. Have you ever had a stranger come to you and tell you something that did not make sense at the moment, but you could not get it out of your mind? Have you ever had someone sit beside you at the bus or train and start talking to you? Curiously, what came out of their mouth was exactly what you needed to hear at that moment. Suddenly that messenger is no longer sitting beside you and you realize that you did not even ask them for their name. We wish to introduce you to "the messengers." They are all around you. (p286) "The Messengers"

98. We wish you to start listening to those messages. They come from spirit and they are designed to give you a hand and direct you through your journey. We see many of you who dismiss these messages as curious or as coincidences. We ask you not to dismiss anything as coincidence. At times, the angels work the night shift so they can play the right song on the radio that gives you a feeling. That feeling may be the key to a resolution for a question that you have been having in your relationships. (p286)

99. You are here to discover who you are and to learn about the divinity inside of you. Some of you choose to discover it through one type of lesson and yet others choose to discover it through another. The role you play changes very quickly. You come and already you have to go back. Only when you are of advanced age do you realize how quickly it all happened. From the perspective of the past, you come closer to the perspective of spirit. From the perspective of age, you see the circle in greater clarity. (p293) "The Tapestry

100. You are here to learn about energy from all possible angles. There is never a judgment on how you use your energy. However, the law of karma is very literal. It is one to one. When you play the game just so you can have the trophy, you miss the point altogether. It is the manner in which you play that scores points recorded on the eternal scoreboard you call your higher self. (p296)

101. Those who remember more and who are awakened are responsible to turn the light on for those who are in darkness. When you are in a group standing in a room and all of you are holding a candle in your hands, when another person joins the group also holding a candle, the amount of light added is quite small and insignificant. Now have the same person enter a room that is full of people, but none of them is holding a candle, and you experience the whole room transform and all those in the room can see. (p300) "Candle in a Dark Room"

102. You come with another angel through contract. Both of you sign with a golden pen to work through the issues and challenges, using love. As you move through the layers, you must face many other emotions, such as anger, hate, jealousy, resentment, etc. You work through these other layers in order to clear them so you can eventually connect through love. The value of the relationships lies in the emotions. Your emotions are the fuel that propels you forward. If there is very little emotional energy exchange, you may not be able to move anywhere. (p304)

103. Time is your teacher, because it serves as a hint to the fact that you are not your body. As you grow old, many of you still feel young and many of you do not match inside what they see in the mirror. You are eternal and time is designed to give you clues to your eternity. You are born and within a short period of time you reach old age. That span of time is your runway. Your greatest, most profound life portion is in the end portion of the runway, where you hopefully gathered enough speed so that your wings take flight. (p308) "The Runway"

104. Time is your friend, as it keeps you in an environment that is ever-changing, so you can learn, at every moment, about you. It is as if you are standing in a room and a lamp is lighting you from one side. That side is your youth. As you turn around slowly, the lamp illuminates a different aspect of you. Why would you not want to see one aspect and

care only for the other? All aspects of you are beautiful and sacred. (p310)

105. You did not come here at this time to be lying in your hammocks, drinking the nectar of heaven. You are the transformers of energy. You are built to bring light to where it is dark. You are the one who trained for this time and dreamt of the opportunity to be here when it all happens. Those of you who are hearing these messages, we ask you to please remember who you are and wake up, because you are the warriors of light. Do you think that you came here to rest? We have news for you. (p314) "Drinking Nectar"

106. You are beautiful and for you to feel the magnificence of you, you must be willing to change. You must be willing to let go of all the darkness, so you can begin to shine your light. You have been sold on many things and those things act as a blanket that obscures your light. You must be ready to change and remove all the layers that keep your light from shining. (p318)

107. There is never a judgment, as you are on a journey of learning the different aspects of yourself. Those aspects are at times difficult and you must come to peace with them as well. We tell you over and over that the one most important attribute on this path is to love yourself, as you are parts and pieces of GOD walking in duality. When you use love with all of your different aspects, your divinity is revealed and you take the hand of spirit and walk the path that you intended to walk. (p321)

Dedication

I WISH TO DEDICATE THIS BOOK to those who give intent to turn on their light and discover their own divinity.

I dedicate this book to all those who are on the path of becoming masters.

I dedicate this book to all those who use the power of love and healing for themselves, for their fellow angels and for mother earth.

I dedicate this book to you.

If you happened to pick this book up and went as far as purchasing it, know that you are one of those who are on a mission described in these pages.

It is no coincidence that you came about this book, as the angels tells us that they can see the potential in each and every one who will ever read these pages. Know that they know your circumstances and can see the potential healing in your life.

Know that you are loved and are never judged no matter where you are on the path. Know that you are blessed for walking the walk of an angel disguised as a human on this beautiful planet, and so be it.

I wish to dedicate this book to my parents who have always encouraged me to be who I am.

And I especially wish to dedicate this book to my wife and daughter who allow me the most wonderful home where I can grow, learn, and understand more about my self and my journey.

I thank you.

Acknowledgments

I LEFT THIS PART to the end as my gratitude is over flowing to all those who were part of this process and played a part in my life while writing and bringing this book to light.

I am eternally grateful for the angels. I can feel you all the time and your love and teachings are a gift that I will always cherish and hold to guide me through my life. I thank you.

I wish to thank the many authors and healers who do the light work for the planet bringing information about love, and our true nature because without you the planet will not be as bright.

With love and appreciation I wish the thank my dear friends with whom I shared this material in the early stages and throughout the process and you know who you are. Your encouragement, support, guidance and love cannot be measured and I am eternally grateful.

I wish to thank my editor Jeff Davis from Center to Page who shared his wisdom and sensitivity and so gracefully showed me the path to bring this book from the center to the page. I wish to thank Peter Lewis who further helped to polish the material in a concise and perceptive manner.

I extend my heartfelt appreciation to my publisher Paul Cohen and designer Georgia Dent from Monkfish/ Epigraph Publishing for their wonderful direction, knowledge, expertise and overall outstanding support and sensitivity in manifesting this book.

I wish to thank my parents for their love and support and for allowing me to grow up in an environment where anything is possible.

I especially wish to extend my deepest gratitude and love to my wife who is my life partner and teacher and to my daughter. Both are my ultimate messengers about love, life and the path of moving forward. You are the pillars of my life and I am grateful for every moment that we share together. I love you both and I always will.

www.andsobeit.com

CPSIA information can be obtained at www.ICGtesting.com
Printed in the USA
265825BV00001B/3/P